Getting Beyond "Hello"

Getting Beyond "Hello"

Miss Mingle's Guide to Navigating the Nineties

Jeanne Martinet
a.k.a. Miss Mingle

A Citadel Press Book
Published by Carol Publishing Group

HM
132
.M346
1996

A Citadel Press Book
Published by Carol Publishing Group
Citadel Press is a registered trademark of Carol Communications, Inc.

Editorial Offices: 600 Madison Avenue, New York, NY 10022
Sales & Distribution Offices: 120 Enterprise Avenue, Secaucus, NJ 07094
In Canada: Canadian Manda Group, One Atlantic Avenue, Suite 105, Toronto, Ontario M6K 3E7, Canada

Queries regarding rights and permissions should be addressed to: Carol Publishing Group, 600 Madison Avenue, New York, NY 10022

Carol Publishing Group Books are available at special discounts for bulk purchases, for sales promotions, fund-raising, or educational purposes. Special editions can also be created to specifications. For details contact: Special Sales Department, Carol Publishing Group, 120 Enterprise Avenue, Secaucus, NJ 07094

Manufactured in the United States of America
12 11 10 9 8 7 6 5 4 3 2 1

Library of Congress Cataloging-in-Publication Data

Martinet, Jeanne, 1958–
    Getting beyond "hello" : Miss Mingle's guide to navigating the nineties / Jeanne Martinet, a.k.a. Miss Mingle.
        p.   cm.
    "A Citadel Press book."
    ISBN 0-8065-1785-9 (pbk.)
    1. Interpersonal relations. 2. Interpersonal communication. 3. Conversation. 4. Etiquette. I. Title.
HM132.M346   1996
302—dc20   95-47093
                                                               CIP

There is no such thing as small talk—only small minds.
—Anonymous

Contents

A Note From Miss Mingle

In January 1993 I received the following letter:

Dear Ms. Martinet:

I read your book The Art of Mingling *from cover to cover and it has really changed my life. I used to be so afraid of going to parties that I would actually get physically ill before every single one of them, which I guess was my subconscious making it impossible for me to go. This was hard on my body as well as on my social life.*

Now, after studying your methods for overcoming "minglephobia" and your instructions on how to handle every kind of mingling situation, I no longer get sick before parties! I mean, I still don't actually go *to any of the parties, but at least I don't get sick anymore.*

I just wanted to write you and thank you.

                                    The Happy Hermit

When *The Art of Mingling* was published in 1992, I must admit I was not completely aware of the amount of mingling-related fear that existed out in the world. I evidently touched a societal nerve. It seems that most people become stuck, stymied, or struck dumb in all kinds of social circumstances and have no road maps to help them through their people-propelled predicaments. In fact, my research shows that a good 90 percent of America has minglephobia (the fear of mingling), or some other painful mingling disorder. It is also apparent that the accompanying level of terror ranks not very far below that involved in public speaking (and in one recent study public speaking ranked higher than death).

Mingling is indeed an art—a delicate, intricate, rich one; filled with psychological pitfalls and cultural rules and rituals—but it is an easy-to-master art if practiced. The trouble is that although we live in a magnified, megabyte world of faxes and E-mail and Websites, instead of getting more adept at communication we are getting less adept. We may live in the communication age, but somewhere along the way we lost the knack of *oral* communication—of standing face to face with someone without shriveling up in a heap of nervous twitches and stammers.

Over the past couple of years, I have received so many letters asking me for more information and for answers to individual mingling problems that I decided these questions would be worth sharing in a separate book. Most of the situations covered herein are similar to ones we all face at some time or another, from dilemmas about rebuffing unwanted suitors to questions about dealing with unruly guests. It is my sincere hope that the practical, field-tested, and easy-to-use techniques and lines contained in Miss Mingle's answers will help you face your next mingling challenge. However, if nothing else, the letters themselves may serve as comfort to insecure minglers everywhere. It may help to know that you are not the only person who feels helpless in the face of many social incidents or terrified at the prospect of an upcoming social function.

Some readers may wonder where the name "Miss Mingle" came from. Believe it or not, after the success of *The Art of Mingling* I was dubbed "Miss Mingle" by several acquaintances. I confess that when people started calling me by this nom de plume, I at first recoiled. (It sounded to me like a cross between a 1930s dance hall hostess, a blue-haired social secretary, and Dame Edna.) But the nickname stuck, as nicknames are apt to, and I must admit that now I am rather proud to be Miss Mingle. Proud because, to tell the truth, I really *have* developed mingling strategies—by trial and error—that rarely fail, and I am delighted to be able to pass these effective tips on to other nervous party-goers and insecure conversationalists.

So listen up, here's the first and most important secret for your mingling success: Enjoy yourself no matter what. That's an order, straight from Miss Mingle.

Acknowledgments

I would like to express my gratitude to everyone who sent letters and allowed them to be included in this book. The questions and problems you were kind enough to share may keep others from having to face unarmed the same kinds of public paralysis, mingling mess, dangerous dilemma, and social scrape you had to. If nothing else, your stories will make readers glad nothing like that has ever happened to *them*. (So far, that is.)

I would also like to thank my talented editor, Kevin McDonough.

Getting
Beyond
"Hello"

The Hell in Hello

When we travel on an airplane, the tensest moment for most of us is during takeoff. We secure our seat belts and try not to think about the fact that most accidents happen as the plane is lifting off the runway. We pretend not to care where the exits are when the flight attendant woodenly points them out. We remind ourselves that the intense revving sound of the motor is normal.

Having a conversation is like flying—the most terrifying part is in the beginning, during the moment we first meet a new person or first greet an old acquaintance. It is in the uncertain moment of "hello" that we feel that anything can happen. We are in completely unknown territory. Will this person like us, snub us, laugh at us, walk away? What if our radar doesn't work, and we don't know where to steer the conversation? What if we crash and burn before we even get off the ground?

Here are some of the most common questions I've received about this super-scary aspect of mingling. Relax: The captain has turned off the FASTEN YOUR SEAT BELT sign.

Dear Miss Mingle:

I have always had trouble remembering people's names. I am in a constant state of panic because I am always running into people whose faces are familiar but whose names escape me. My father, who has been a salesman for thirty years, told me I should just do what he does, which is to march right up, stick out his hand and confidently give his own name. The other person, my father explained, will then automatically offer his or her own name.

I tried to use this trick last week with disastrous consequences. Having suddenly found myself face to face with a man I had met at least twice before at business conferences, I put my hand out with the required bravado, smiled, and announced my own name, "John H_____."
The man looked at me and said "I'm not John H_____!"
and stalked off.
Is this a stupid trick or did I just do it wrong?

Feeling Stupid

Dear Feeling Stupid:

Don't feel bad. Forgetting people's names is one of the world's most common mingling afflictions. I once got so nervous that I forgot my own name and introduced myself as the person who had just introduced herself to me. (You should have seen the bewildered look on her face.)

As for your daddy's handy-dandy introduction trick, it's not a bad little gambit, especially in its proper form, which is, "Perhaps you remember me, I'm John H_____." (not just "John H_____!"). However, it is fairly transparent and therefore only appropriate in a situation where it is excusable for you to have forgotten the person's name. By introducing yourself, you indicate that reintroductions are necessary. Translation: I don't remember your name.

There are many other effective ways to smooth over this awkward moment of temporary amnesia, ranging from sheepish honesty ("I really am horrible with names—I'm surprised I remember my own.") to hyperbole ("Well hello, *darling!*"). My own preferred course of action is to say something like "Hi, I was hoping I'd see you here," or "Well, look who it is! Hullo!" and avoid the subject of names altogether. The other person, who has more than likely forgotten your name, too, will be forever in your debt.

Dear Miss Mingle:

What is it with this kissing business? Many of my old friends and acquaintances—who years ago wouldn't dream of such familiarity—suddenly want to kiss me every time we meet. I've tried turning away my face and just hugging, but it is awkward to end up being kissed on your ear or on the top of your head. I hate to insult friends, but I do not really want to be kissed.

Kissed-Off

Dear Kissed-Off:

I'm with you. I like to reserve my kissing for times of true affection (or passion). I'm not sure how all this superficial smooching got started, but I can't help thinking somehow the French are to blame.

The ridiculous thing about the Greeting Kiss is that, since nobody really wants to be kissing everybody all the time, what you end up with is a lot of "faux" kissing (where you just put your cheeks together while one of you makes a quiet kissing noise) or out-and-out "air kissing," which is very silly and smacks (!) of insincerity. Worst of all, since hello-kissing has become an expected social convention, when a good friend who you might not mind kissing arrives at the same time as someone you don't like, you may actually end up kissing the disliked person! Kissing people you don't even enjoy *talking* to can really tie your soul in knots and is just plain bad for you.

You should certainly never be expected to kiss someone *on the lips* unless you really want to (not in this country, anyway). After all, lip kissing is unhygienic and extremely intimate. Also it can smear your lipstick. In order to avoid kisses aimed at your lips, simply present a cheek to the kiss perpetrator. But if cheek kissing bothers you too, here is some antikissing artillery:

1. Make excuses. Say "I've got garlic breath, you don't want to kiss me," or "Don't kiss me—I think I'm catching a cold." Of course, this ploy has drawbacks. If you use an excuse of this type every time you see a person, he will either begin to think you are a hypochondriac or he will start to get suspicious.

2. Get your mate or date to play defense for you. This is tricky and may need to be practiced. The idea is for your "teammate" to get in between you and the potential kisser, while you busy yourself hanging up coats and saying things like "Come in, come in! Go on in to the living room, please."

3. Before the other person can make a move, you say, "Hello! Give me a big hug!" I have found that people respond very well to specific instructions during social transitions, such as when they are entering or exiting. Now, occasionally they will kiss you *as well* as hug you (especially if they really liked the hug), but not often. Remember that a lot of other people besides you are secretly standoffish about this hello-goodby kissing thing, and will welcome an escape in the form of a hug request. If you are too bashful to *specify* a hug, you may have to (in spite of your uneasiness about where a misfired kiss may end up on your person) resort to turning your head as far away as you can from the person's lips, thereby forcibly transforming the Greeting Kiss into the Greeting Hug. And always make sure to dispel any hurt feelings about the unavailability of your facial area with a hearty "It's *so* great to see you!" afterward.

If none of these defense systems seems to work for you, there's not much else you can do except to look forward to the time when your friends are all too old to make the effort.

Dear Miss Mingle:

I attend many cocktail parties and other functions where name badges are worn. My problem is that I'm nearsighted, even with glasses, and often can't see the other person's name, although they can usually see mine. I feel it's creepy to lean too close (especially with women, since I'm a man) for a look, so here's my question: Should I just say, "Hey, I'm blind, what's your name?" Should I give up on using the person's name? Or should I engage in an occasional lecherous lean?

Please hurry up with your answer. The convention season is coming up.

Cockeyed at Cocktails

Dear Cockeyed:

While I am generally in favor of lecherous leans, if I were you I would just ignore the name tag altogether and introduce myself as if there were none. (I hate name tags anyway because they eliminate the easiest opening remark possible: Here's who *I* am, who are *you*?) If you just go ahead and say your own name—in spite of its being plastered on your chest—the other person will more than likely tell you her name. If not, you can always declare that you never read people's badges because you feel they're gauche. And, in fact, in Miss Mingle's opinion, they are.

Dear Miss Mingle:

My husband never introduces me to people he knows when we meet them unexpectedly. He claims he just can't remember their names under the "pressure, " but it makes me feel incredibly ill at ease. What should I do?

Clueless

Dear Clueless:

Just last week I was out with a good friend and we bumped into an acquaintance of hers (and he was a good-looking guy, darn it!) to whom she failed to introduce me. In general, people *don't* do this on purpose; their own fears or self-absorption causes them to either forget the person's name or simply to forget to introduce you. In times past, when people had better manners, introduction etiquette was so ingrained in them that nothing could derail them. But alas, that is a bygone era.

There is a simple answer to this dilemma: Introduce yourself. If your husband has already started talking to the mystery person, just wait for a slight pause and stick your hand out toward him. If you and your husband have the same name, you can say, "Hello, I'm

Judy [husband's surname]," which is a little more subtle than announcing, "Hi, I'm his wife."

Warning: Don't wait too long before introducing yourself; after about three minutes it becomes a much more cumbersome task.

Dear Miss Mingle:

While mingling with your mate is one of the joys of being in a relationship, I have a bit of an etiquette problem. How does one introduce part of a same-sex couple? I'm always nonplussed when it comes to introducing my "boyfriend"—after all, I am forty-three years old! He's more than a "lover" or "partner;" I refuse to use the sterile-sounding "significant other," and the obituary term "companion" has too much an air of death about it.

Also, how does one introduce a same-sex couple to someone else, if you want to indicate they are together. (This is Bob and his wife, Linda, and this is Joe and his _____, Tony)?

At a Loss for Words

Dear At a Loss:

This quite frequent problem is not exclusively a gay one; it's really about not being "married." At the risk of sounding radical, anyone who does not fit into the traditional patriarchal system (even a man and woman who live together in a committed relationship but have not asked the church or state to sanctify their union) has the very same introduction difficulties. There are no words that mean wife or husband except for those words. One of the reasons you are having trouble finding substitute words is because it is, in fact, not necessarily natural to claim ownership of another person ("This is *my* wife...."). In many ways relationships are in the process of being redefined, and these kinds of uncomfortable social moments are the growing pains of our new relationships.

However, let me get down off my soapbox and offer you some practical suggestions. If you want to take the easiest and safest route, you can simply introduce people by their names alone (if you can remember them): "Linda and Bob, this is Joe and Tony." Why not let people figure out what the couple's connection is to each other for themselves, during the ensuing conversation? However, if you are more comfortable using a title of some sort, or if the situation seems to demand descriptions, choose one of the many alternatives to *boyfriend* in the following list. They range from the acceptable to the more adventuresome. The most important thing to remember is that if you are introducing a heterosexual and a homosexual couple at the same time, try to introduce them using similar designations.

Alternative Labels for Lovers

partner	woman
mate	man
spouse	womanfriend

friend
companion
paramour
lover
soul mate
lover, best friend,
    etc.
beau
steady
live-in
consort
darling
sweetheart
honey
beloved
honey bunch
sweetie-pie

manfriend
old man
old lady
other half
better half
love

flame
roommate for life
squeeze
main squeeze
love-slave
snuggle-bunny
bed buddy
eternal playmate
future-Ex
the love of my/his/her life

Perils of Apparel

Among the niceties of times past was the certainty of a strict dress code. Invitations always stated "Semiformal" or "Black Tie," and rules of etiquette were such that on most occasions one knew exactly what kind of thing to wear. Of course, a lot of people couldn't afford the correct attire, but at least they knew what was what.

Unfortunately, we now exist in a kind of twilight zone of clothing conventions: We have freed ourselves from the tyranny of rigid rules, but most of us are not emancipated enough to be unfazed when we show up conspicuously over- or underdressed. Perhaps sometime in the future, we will have gotten to the point where it is acceptable to wear ball gowns to the park and jeans to a church wedding; but somehow, I doubt it. Clothing is part of the language of community, and fashion is not just the expression of the self but the expression of the group as a whole. When you are dressed "wrong" you feel that you are somehow not a part of the group; you can feel uncertain and off balance. In fact, the expression "out of kilter" was probably coined by a Scotsman who showed up somewhere in a pair of pants.

Dear Miss Mingle:

My husband and I had planned to go out to dinner with another couple one evening. It was the other couple who made the reservations—at one of their favorite restaurants. When they arrived to pick us up, it was obvious that—compared to them—we were overdressed for the occasion. They took one look at us and then one of them said, "Are we dressed too casual for you?"

Of course, what they meant was that we were too dressed up for them. I realize I should have asked in advance what to wear, but most of the restaurants in our area are pretty fancy. (How was I to know they had made reservations at a burger place?) Should we have gone upstairs and changed our clothes? And what could I have said in response to their snide comment?

All Gussied Up

Dear All Gussied Up:

Rule of dress number one: *Never assume.* Next time, ask your friends where you are going so that you can more properly judge the clothing requirements. Or inquire point blank what you should wear. Asking for instructions may not seem like a "cool" way to behave, but, on the other hand, there is nothing particularly cool about showing up at a party in a chiffon and sequin dress when everyone else is in bathing suits.

Rule of dress number two: *In general, it is better to be overdressed than underdressed.* A tuxedo at a soccer game can give you the mysterious air of someone who has fancier places to go later on, while sweats at an awards ceremony only look clownish and awkward. So if you had to err, at least it was in the right direction.

Rule of dress number three: *Never make someone else feel uncomfortable about their level, quality, or style of dress.* Doing this is the height of bad manners and shows a hidden insecurity. A good comeback for your rude friend's "Are we dressed toooo casual for you?" might have been an airy, "No, not at all. I'm sure *you* two would look fine even in overalls!" (Moral: Sometimes a backhanded compliment is the fastest way to put the ball back in the other person's court.)

Dear Miss Mingle:

The MOST embarrassing thing happened to me last month. I was invited to a very special party—an engagement party for a friend of mine. It was held at a very nice club, and I bought a new dress just for the occasion. (In all modesty, I have to tell you I really looked great in it!) But when I arrived at the party, I was shocked to see that not one but two other women were wearing the exact same dress I was! I was so horrified that I could hardly talk to anyone, much less "sparkle" as I had wanted to in my new threads. Is there anything I could have done to have gotten past this nightmare, short of stripping down in the ladies room?

Carbon Copy

Dear Carbon Copy:

It is not that unusual for two people to be accidentally dressed in the same outfit, though I must say I have never heard of three. Still, my advice to you would be to try not to take it so seriously. It is, after all, a rather humorous situation, once you get past the disturbing feeling of seeing other people in *your* clothes.

You might have easily turned the coincidence to your advantage and made it a mingling asset rather than a detriment. For instance, you could have concocted a fun story to tell people about why the three of you were dressed identically (that you heard you had to wear this exact dress to get into the party; that you are sisters separated at birth who just rediscovered each other that night; that you all model for the same designer; that you are going to swap lives with each other before the end of the night; or that the outfit is the uniform of a new religious sect). Even better, you could have gotten together with your party look-alikes and decided collectively what amusing explanation you were going to use.

If making up stories is not your style, you can still make the predicament work for you instead of against you. Rather than running and hiding behind a column, go put your arms around the other women and congratulate them on their good taste! It's a great way to meet at least two new people at the party (you have a guaranteed opening line) as long as you adopt a playful attitude rather than an embarrassed one. And where is the great shame in showing up in the same thing as someone else anyway? Very few people at any social event are actually wearing originals. You wouldn't catch a man going all funny on you because someone across the room is wearing the same navy blue suit.

Dear Miss Mingle:

Recently I took a friend out to see a Broadway show for his birthday. I was dressed in a coat and tie, but when I went to collect the "birthday boy," he was dressed in an old pair of pants and a stained polo shirt. I have to say I was a little offended. After all, I was taking him to a show, and it was his birthday—a special occasion as far as I was concerned. I realize people don't "dress" for the theater anymore (which I think is a shame), but I felt as if my friend's sloppy attire was a statement about what he thought about me. He just didn't make the effort to try to look nice. I almost made a comment, but I held my tongue. What should I have said, if anything? And how can I now (after the fact) let him know about the message he sends by his choice of clothing?

Dressed Up and Teed Off

Dear Dressed Up:

I can sympathize with you in more ways than one. I hate going to the opera and sitting next to someone in shorts and a T-shirt; it makes me feel as though I am having an extremely bad dream. The fact is that people have widely different ideas today about what type of clothing is to be worn where. And while it is for the most part a good thing that people are freer to express themselves in this way than they ever have been before, it does tend to create the kind of confusion and hurt feelings you write about. Try not to take it personally. Many people just love comfort or don't have a clue as to what's appropriate, or both.

Next time, say something to your friend like, "And let's get dressed up a little, just for fun, okay?" or tease him: "And by the way, I want to see you wearing something from your A-list this time!" (Please note: Do be certain the poor man actually *owns* these mythical clothes before you request them.)

Dear Miss Mingle:

A funny thing happened to me on the way to the costume party. The back of my pants (I was going as a 1920s gangster) got caught on the door of the cab as I was getting out and ripped from the waistline to the knee. Basically, those pants were history. I wanted to get right back in the cab, go home, and change; but alas, I was with my wife, who thought the whole thing was hilarious (so did the cab driver). During the party, I tried to keep my coat over the pants, but it didn't work too well, and, in spite of it being Halloween, I was uncomfortable at having my underwear hanging out there for everyone to see. I'm not too quick on my feet when it comes to these things. What should I have done?

Overexposed

Dear Overexposed:

First of all, one must always carry safety pins (or get one's wife to)—especially when wearing a costume. The safety pin is the handiest thing ever invented. Second, always wear attractive, nonholey underwear (as your mother was always telling you)—just in case. And third, always be prepared to be flexible. In this case, your costume of a 1920s gangster simply became that of a 1920s gangster who had just had a narrow, pants-ripping escape from the law.

Dear Miss Mingle:

I have an urgent question concerning shoes. For years now it's been accepted behavior to wear one's walking shoes (tennis shoes) and carry one's good shoes (usually heels) until you get wherever you're going: the office, a party, whatever. This makes a lot of sense, especially in bad weather, and I'm all for it. But the other day I arrived at a dinner party and could not find a place in the lobby to sit down and switch my footwear. I decided I would make the switch after I got off the elevator, before entering the host's apartment. I didn't realize the elevator opened up directly into the apartment! So there I was in my cocktail dress and my muddy Avias for all to see. What is correct shoe-removal etiquette in a case like this?

Footloose and Uptight

Dear Footloose and Uptight:

Next time, don't let on you feel anything but completely normal and at ease. Smile confidently as if nothing is wrong. When the host shows you where to put your coat (hopefully in another room) you can sit down and change your shoes there. If the host offers to take your coat for you, or he indicates that there is no separate location for coats (or you are not *wearing* a coat), just ask him quietly if there is some place where you could change your shoes. Any host worth his salt will help you make a smooth and unobtrusive footwear transition.

Dear Miss Mingle:

The other night, when I was at an office party, I happened to mention to this one woman that I really liked her dress and I would love to know where she had gotten it. She looked at me kind of strangely and said, "I don't remember," and then she walked away. Somehow I had offended her, but I swear I don't know how. I really <u>did</u> like her dress, and it seemed natural to comment on it. By the *way, it was a black cocktail dress with a high neck in the front and a low V in the back.*

Miss Mingle, what did I do wrong?

Making the Wrong Fashion Statement

Dear M.T.W.F.S:

It sounds as if the woman read something into your comment that you did not mean. She may have thought you were being insincere or sarcastic. She might have been feeling in some way insecure about her dress, and your comment made her feel that more keenly. Perhaps the dress was given to her by someone important to her who she lost recently. Or maybe someone else had just told her the back of her dress was too low to be wearing at an office party. She might have even been afraid you would go out and buy the same dress. You will probably never know the reason for the woman's behavior.

There are, however, some simple guidelines to follow when it comes to flattering someone's attire: Try to limit your comments to accessories—preferably above-the-chest items like earrings or scarves—they are less personal and therefore less likely tooo give offense. And asking where someone got something is a bit too intrusive if you want to be on the safe side, which is certainly the side you want to be on at any office function.

****

Clothes-Lines*

(For the inappropriately dressed)

Too Formal:

"I always like to dress up. For me, life is one big formal ball!"

"Excuse the dress [suit], I'm meeting someone later and I won't have a minute to change!"

"I just felt dressy tonight!" (accompany this line with a flourish or twirl)

"I wonder when everyone else is changing into their *real* party clothes."

Too Informal:

"I know this is a bit casual, but everything I own seems to be at the cleaners this week. I've just *got* to get a new personal assistant!"

"Do you like this wild outfit? It's just my way of saying The heck with skirts and heels!"

"My luggage was stolen."

"It's a Thoreau thing."

Just Plain Wrong:

"In case you are wondering why I am wearing these _____ [fishing boots, overalls, spurs], a friend of mine—who shall remain nameless—bet me that I wouldn't have the guts."

"You won't believe this, but someone played a practical joke on me and told me this was a costume party."

* Always remember that there is no law that says you *must* explain your appearance; use a clothes-line only if you feel it will alleviate embarrassment. Some people like to tough it out in silence.

****

Identity Crises: To Lie or Not to Lie

To lie, or not to lie: that is the question: Whether 'tis nobler in mingling to suffer the slings and arrows of people who are unimpressed by your profession or repulsed by your circumstances; or to take arms against a sea of troubles, and by a little fibbing end them?

Dear Miss Mingle:

I meet a lot of agents and producers, and sometimes they ask me what I've done in show business. The real answer is that I've written for and performed in every medium but still have to work the graveyard shift as a typist. My wife, who usually happens to be standing nearby in these situations, tends to let the cat out of the bag, whereupon the agent or producer knits his brow, purses his lips, and very gently and slowly snorts. He then resumes the conversation, but it's like he's in another building somewhere.

I don't really want to lie about my past (not because it's immoral, but for fear of being found out and humiliated). All the same, I wonder if there isn't some vague way I could suggest that rather than having leprosy I am on the cusp of phenomenal wealth and celebrity, and the agent has lucked out in standing next to me. I don't care about the ethical aspects of it, just the success rate.

Bitterly Obscure

Dear Bitterly Obscure:

First of all, what's up with your wife? Why does she feel moved to humiliate you in front of an important contact? Tell her to go mingle in a separate part of the room, for gosh sakes, or to stick to disclosing embarrassing things about her *own* life.

As for being nervous about lying, remember that in the entertainment business lying is the norm. Agents and producers swim daily in a fetid sea of exaggerations, half-truths, and wholesale fabrications. You are right that there is nothing morally wrong with lying while mingling, especially if it makes you feel better during an interaction. After all, we are not talking about falsifying official records, just a little superficial prevarication. Of course, the spiritually healthy path would be one of unabashed honesty and openness about all aspects of one's life. But if you were spiritually healthy you probably wouldn't be mingling with agents.

The real trick is (for, as you say, the only really important thing is not being caught) to exaggerate in such a way that if someone does come up to you in the middle of your description of your exciting acting career and inquires about your boring night job, you don't look like a pathetic fake who is trying to be somebody you are not. For the best kind of truth stretching, follow these simple rules:

1. Lie by omission, not by assertion. Just don't mention irrelevant parts of your life, like, for instance, the fact that you have worked for the last three years at K Mart.

2. If, while you're talking with the agent, another person does happen to ask you how your work down at K Mart is going, look confused at first, then laugh and say something like, "I'm not doing that too much anymore. I'll have to catch you up to speed sometime soon." (Big, confident smile here, as you resume talking to the agent, turning your back on the unwelcome intruder.) "You've found out about my sordid past. Everyone should work at K Mart once in their life—it's a real education. Now, what were we talking about?"

3. If someone does completely blow your cover, so that it is obvious to the agent that you really *do* currently work pretty much full-time at K Mart, *do not* behave as

if you have been "outed." Don't wince, don't even blink. Just continue talking about what you've accomplished in acting and writing. If the agent doesn't realize that many geniuses have had lowly jobs before they became famous, he or she is probably not a good agent anyway.

On the other hand, if you are at a social event where you are sure *no one* knows you (and you can put a muzzle on your wife), you're home free. Lie, lie, lie. Have a field day. But don't go overboard. It takes one to know one, and agents are pretty good at sniffing out a fraud.

Dear Miss Mingle:

I am a hardworking housewife, proud of the fact that I am an "at home mom." But whenever I am out somewhere and a woman doctor or lawyer (or other type of career woman) asks, "And what do you do?" I always wish I had a terrific new way to say "I'm a housewife." Any suggestions?

Please Don't Call Me Domestic Engineer

Dear Please Don't Call Me:

Housewife really *is* a horrible word. After all, are you married to the house? (Or are you only a wife when you are actually *in* the house?) And what condescending jerk invented the term "domestic engineer" anyway? It sounds like a title you give to a first grader along with a hat and a badge. Language always reflects society, and most other terms for housewife tend to belittle the intense amount of work and care that goes into caring for a family and a home.

It is this very common conversational concern among married women that inspires most of them to cluster together (for safety) at parties. However, here are a few fun answers to that inevitable what-do-you-do question:

"I'm a live-in housekeeper, gourmet chef, child psychologist, tutor, bookkeeper, and paramour."

"I take care of our three children and keep my husband organized. A lot of overtime, but I love the people I work with!"

"I'm a love-slave. In other words, a housewife."

"I usually don't tell people this, but since you look so trustworthy...I pose as an ordinary housewife but am really doing top secret work for the government."

"For the last several years I've been working on having a nervous breakdown."

Dear Miss Mingle:

I used to be an interesting person, always able to engage anyone in fascinating conversation. Now that I'm a full-time mom (and loving every minute of it), I find that on those rare occasions when I can get out without milk on my blouse or Big Bird in my handbag, I preface most of my remarks with "I used to." The rest of my comments have to do with children (in particular or in general) and child-rearing. Help! How can I become more interesting at parties—without abandoning my current lifestyle?

Just Somebody's Mom

Dear Just Somebody's Mom:

Be proud, walk tall, hold your head high! Your career as a mother is probably more interesting than a lot of "real" careers, and frankly, very few careers make for more than about five or ten minutes of interesting conversation anyway. You live in the world the same as anyone else. Talk about the school system; ask people if they believe in sending kids to psychologists, ballet before age three, or throwing infants into swimming pools to teach them to swim; talk about your struggle for higher self-esteem; talk about changes in your neighborhood, trips you'd like to take, the environment, or the latest Elvis craze.

If you were fascinating before you became a full-time mom, there is no reason you can't be fascinating now. (It's not *who* you are it's *how* you are.) Just don't talk about dirty diapers, baby food, play dates, or Barney.

Dear Miss Mingle:

I recently broke my arm in a most embarrassing fashion. I was fighting with my brother. He pushed me down, my arm hit a pipe, and snap went the bone.

I'm sure you assume from the above statement that I am

a child or a teenager, but I am a forty-eight-year-old man (and my brother is fifty-three!). People see the cast and the sling and naturally ask me what happened. It's humiliating to go into the embarrassing details, especially over and over again. I know everyone is trying to be nice, but I'd really like to avoid the subject altogether.

What do I tell people who ask about my arm?

Sheepish in Sheepshead Bay

Dear Sheepish:

You have four choices:

1. You can wear a big sign on your chest that says PLEASE DON'T ASK ME ABOUT MY ARM.

2. You can tell people the true story—the short or long version—the short (and slightly watered-down) version being simply, "My brother and I were horsing around and I broke my arm."

3. You can lie. I often recommend lying as the easiest, safest, and most interesting course of action. A cast is actually a great mingling prop. It gives everyone something to talk about and allows you prepare witty remarks in advance. As long as no one present knows the truth, you can be as creative as you like. Tell people you fell off a yacht at Bar Harbor (the Glamorous Lie); tell them you were climbing a childhood tree to see if a sweetheart's initials you had once carved were still there (the Romantic Lie); tell them it is job-related, but you are not supposed to talk about it (the Mysterious

Lie); tell them you fell off the roof of the Plaza Hotel and landed on top of a horse and buggy (the Outrageous Lie). An interesting lie can turn your mingling problem into an asset.

4. Better yet: *Admit* that you don't want to say how you broke your arm because the truth is too horribly embarrassing. This is called "the tease" among veteran minglers, and will make almost anyone desperate to know the truth—which you, of course, will not tell them. (The secret to the tease is that you must *never* give in to the pressure to reveal the truth.) The result of this clever ploy is that you will be surrounded by people constantly trying to guess how you broke your arm. This makes for fun conversation and ensures your party popularity.

In fact, now that I think of it, I may just go out and get a cast put on my *own* arm.

About Poise

For me the word poise conjures up images of Jackie Kennedy, a woman who never appeared to be ruffled. She always spoke in that special calm, quiet manner. She never seemed to need anything from anybody. Poise—that certain inner balance and aura of self-containment—is a person's best friend at any social gathering. Poise will make you seem at home wherever you are. Poise will draw others to you.

Some people have poise naturally (or, in the new vernacular, they are "centered"), and these people are indeed to be envied. The shocking truth about poise, however, is that most people are only faking it. (Shhh.... And you can too.)

Dear Miss Mingle:

Generally I am quite comfortable in social situations and am quite at ease when meeting new people. However, there is one situation that I found quite daunting.

Recently, I attended a cocktail party where the hostess was the only person I knew. On my arrival she was nowhere to be seen. All the other guests seemed to know each other and were intently engaged in conversation. I felt extremely conspicuous and uncomfortable and found it awkward to mingle with the crowd.

Could you make some suggestions to save me from such embarrassment again?

Stranger in a Strange Land

Dear Stranger:

The important thing to remember in a situation like this is that it is not *your fault* that you don't know anyone there. It doesn't mean you have no friends, or that you are a social outcast; you are merely in foreign territory. Take a deep breath. Nothing spectacular is expected of you under the circumstances. You cannot really fail, because facing a room full of total strangers is beyond the call of duty even for experienced minglers. Anything short of turning around and leaving is a personal triumph. Look at it as an exhilarating challenge, "the experts only" slope of social situations. In order to get you started, to take that first push-off down the hill, it may help to use the following Minglephobic's Survival Fantasy:

Pretend you are an international operative, working undercover in a foreign country. Make believe that part of your assignment is to attend this party and to find the other spy—who is also working undercover. While your cover persona is someone who doesn't know anyone and is hoping to make new acquaintances, underneath you are totally confident, sophisticated, worldly, and in control. This party is child's play to you. You put your coat down and begin making chitchat with as many people as you can. (Introduce yourself and ask people how they know the hostess, for starters.) As Natasha, or Boris, the secret agent, you will be exuding confidence and poise. You will even have a little "I've got a secret" glint in your eye, a glint that will give you an attractive, mysterious air.

If you don't care for thrillers, create any fantasy that works for you. The scenario doesn't matter; what's important is that you use any means necessary to trick yourself out of your terror. No one ever has to know you are playing a role, and you can drop the fantasy as soon as you get over your initial discomfort. In fact, you should be sure to come out of your secret fantasy after no longer than an hour, or it could get dangerous. (This technique is not recommended for anyone who has been treated for any type of psychosis. And if you find yourself speaking with a foreign accent, abort the fantasy *immediately*.)

If fantasizing doesn't appeal to you (although I recommend it highly since it is also good for your imagination muscles), try to keep the following mingling fact in mind at all times: Even though you may feel incredibly self-conscious, no one else is going to notice your being ill at ease (unless you stutter, cry, or spill something on them) because they are all too worried about themselves. There is truly nothing to fear but fear itself.

Dear Miss Mingle:

Every time I see this certain girl at a party I really lose my cool. No other girl does this to me. I am usually totally able to smooth talk and charm my way around, but when I see this girl I get paralyzed. I start sweating a lot and I say stupid things like "Howse it gowin?" How can I stabilize, if you know what I mean? I don't want her to think I am a bama.

> *Spazzing Out in Spokane*

Dear Spazzing Out:

I'm not sure anything will really help you—as there are some things in the universe (like biology) that are forces unto themselves—but I read once about a trick men used to use to maintain their composure in situations like yours. Every time you look at this beautiful girl, think to yourself, "What a beautiful horse." The idea is (I think) that if you can imagine this girl as something other than a girl, it will give you some emotional distance. However, I have no concrete evidence that this actually works. Do let me know.

Dear Miss Mingle:

I usually find myself at parties making a big effort to introduce myself to people, initiate conversations, and keep them going by asking lots of questions. Meanwhile, I admire and envy those cool, calm, and collected people who appear content to just hang out whether or not anyone is talking to them—people who always seem to let others ask all the questions while they remain in the more comfortable and easier position of only having to respond.

What can you recommend to help me become a more relaxed mingler? In other words, how can I train myself to stop trying so hard at parties, and start allowing other people to initiate conversations with me?

Over-Eager Beaver

Dear Over-Eager Beaver:

You're right, the most intriguing individuals at any party are the ones who look as if they are not trying at all. In fact, it is a mingling myth that the best conversationalist is the one who continually asks a lot of questions of other people. Being an "interviewer" may make you a great human being, but it usually does not make you popular at parties. What you really want is poise.

The first step to attaining poise is to *pretend* you have it. (It's no accident that the word *poise* is so similar to the word *pose*.) It's actually a matter of a *po*sitive attitude, which is why the following mingling strategy is a spiritually beneficial exercise as well as a socially beneficial one.

Let's say you have just arrived at a crowded party. Perhaps you are feeling nervous, not quite equal to the task of approaching a lot of strangers and trying to get them to talk to you. Here's what you do: Take several deep, slow breaths. Force yourself to move leisurely, as if you are at home in your own garden with the sun on your face; put your coat down; and go get a drink, some food, whatever you want. Keep a pleasant expression on your face (but don't grin or—heaven forbid—giggle). Move around the room and examine the pictures on the wall, the furniture, the drapes, the hors d'oeuvres. Focus intently on whatever you see. Tell yourself that your ultimate happiness does not depend on conversation with anyone in the room. Be calm, and be genuinely interested in what's going on around you.

Here's the tricky part: Once you have attained this high level of self-sufficient self-composure, you have got to also make yourself open for others to approach you. Start to give your attention to the other people at the party. Begin making eye contact with people when you can. Smile warmly, confidently, but not for too long if you don't know the person. Your unspoken message should be, "It would probably be nice to talk to you, and, if you feel like talking to me, I'm here." To help you accomplish the psychological transformation from a needy guest to a nonchalant one, tell yourself that you don't really *need* anyone, but that you *like* everyone.

If you keep these thoughts in your mind and a pleasant expression on your face, people *will* come to you. And you will be amazed at the sense of power it gives you.

Pitching Woo: Mingling for Romance

People are always asking me to tell them the best way to approach a man or the best way to pick up women. "How can I flirt without being too obvious?" "How can I let someone know when I am really interested (or when I am not)?" Almost everyone would like to know how to turn that first meeting into a first date.

Mingling with the idea of hooking up with someone romantically is a very specialized subset of mingling. It is much more psychologically complicated than mere mingling because it has to do not only with the art of conversation, but also with that vast area known as "relationships." It is for this reason that thousands of books have been written about dating and mating: books about communication between the sexes, about commitment, about infidelity, about human sexuality, about changing roles and changing morality, about sexual power politics, about past-life issues, about gender bending, and about healing the romantic self.

Notwithstanding all this well-intentioned analytical hullabaloo, I prefer to think of the initial meeting between two destined-to-be-intertwined people as simply "that old black magic." Nevertheless, there *is* a certain conversational choreography involved in the human mating dance; and while romance is certainly best when it happens naturally, it never hurts to give nature a boost in the form of a preplanned opening line or strategy.

Dear Miss Mingle:

I have such a hard time meeting men. I never meet any at work, so I have been trying to go to events—readings, coffee houses, community meetings, even church gatherings. I know it sounds like a cliché, but often I end up sitting or standing by myself, wondering why men aren't talking to me. I just don't know what to say to someone I don't know, and I am afraid it will be obvious I am there to find a man. Please help!

World's Worst Wallflower

Dear WWW:

Cheer up, you are about to get some good news: About 75 percent of the people at the events you describe feel exactly the same way you do. If you can keep this thought in your mind it will help you a lot. We all believe we are the only ones who feel fear and loneliness, but most people feel these things at least some of the time.

Facing a room full of strangers is like facing a freezing cold swimming pool: You just have to jump in. It's shocking at first, but then you get used to it. It might help take the pressure off to tell yourself you can leave anytime you want to. Then take a deep breath and walk up to someone (don't limit yourself to talking to men; you can meet men through other women), and—if simply introducing yourself doesn't suit you—try one of the following opening lines:

"I was supposed to meet a friend here who didn't show up. Now, like Blanche Dubois, I must depend on the kindness of strangers."

"Isn't this great?"

"Hi. I'm very interested to know what other people think of this _____ [event/evening/meeting/reading/performance]. Do you mind my asking you?"

"Come here seldom?"

* *

First Meeting No-No's

There is a time and place for everything. During that first conversation, you should *never* say:

"You didn't really *wear* that here, did you?"

"I'm usually in much better shape than this."

"So how do you feel about marriage [having kids]?"

"Can you hear my biological clock ticking?"

"People call me the Italian Stallion."

"I'd love for you to meet my parents sometime."

"I'd love for my parents to meet you sometime."

"Everyone thinks I need therapy, but I don't."

"I really like kinky sex."

* *

Dear Miss Mingle:

How do you determine the status (straight, single, interested?) of someone you have just met? And how do you subtly inform someone whether you are in a position to be pursued, or are unavailable, or prefer the other gender? I have heard there are secret signals involving earrings or key chains, but that kind of thing wouldn't appeal to me even if it applied to me, which I don't think it does.

On the Lookout for Love

Dear On the Lookout for Love:

In my opinion, using signals for this sort of thing in contemporary Western society is extremely risky. Like the person at the auction who was just trying to scratch his nose, you could end up sending a signal you never intended. However, if you are in a sociosexual group where a strict and unilateral secret signaling system exists, it certainly does facilitate the whole sticky problem of letting your preferences and availability be known. Most cultures have been using signals of this sort for centuries. (The Hopi Indian women wore their hair a certain way if they wanted to get married; the Pennsylvania Dutch used to paint the gatepost blue to advertise that a girl of marriageable age lived within.)

In the modern world things are fuzzier, but still manageable. Married men are the easiest to flush out. If their ring fingers don't tell you right away, they usually do. Most married men, when they find out you are single, seem to feel an urgent need to let you know they are taken (maybe they think it will keep them safe from their own temptations?)—whether you have shown interest or not. Within the first ten minutes of conversation, they will usually find a way to say something like, "Well, my wife believes that..." or "I was just walking down that street with my wife the other day..." If they don't, they are probably on the prowl, and, unfortunately, you may find out too late.

Gay men and women are sometimes very hard to tell about, and I've heard many a sad story from straight women friends that ended with "And then, after all that, I found out he was gay!" A good test might be to try to see if the person recognizes the name of a writer of gay fiction or of a gay rights activist. Another indication might be if the person is over thirty-five and has a "roommate." But none of this is foolproof. The best aide you have is your own radar, which will usually tell you a lot. People who are gay seem to have a finer honed radar system, maybe because they've had to. (A gay friend of mine calls this "gaydar.")

As for sending out the right vibes to others, there have been many books written on the subject of flirting. I find it fairly easy to let people know my sexual preferences by interjecting something into the conversation like, "Where are all the gorgeous waiters when you need them?" or "I've always loved Paul Newman. If he were single, I'd marry him." Letting someone know you are single and interested is a more delicate matter. The interested part should be unspoken, at least at first; the other person should become aware of your interest merely by your warm attention. However, I usually manage to announce my singlehood by working "As a single woman, I often experience..." into the dialogue.

WARNING: No matter what precautions you take or advice you listen to, it is easy to make mistakes these days. I once met a charming, bearded, deep-voiced man who, at the end of our third date, announced that he was a transsexual. Rather confused, I stammered, "You mean...you want to become a woman?"

He looked at me scornfully. "No, of course not! I was born a woman. I am becoming a man."

My head was spinning for weeks.

Dear Miss Mingle:

I understand that a great place to meet romantic prospects is at those new café-bookstores. But how do I actually begin a conversation with other book browsers? And what are the best sections in which to meet someone I might like? Should I start in the coffee bar?

Reading Between the Lines

Dear Reading Between the Lines:

Bookstores are great mingling places; I know of at least two happy couples who met in bookstores. Obviously, the safest and most natural course of action is for you to hang out in the section of the bookstore *you* enjoy the most. You do, after all, ultimately want to meet someone with interests similar to yours; and in familiar territory you won't be at a loss for words. Also, the object of your attention will be less likely to discover your secret date-seeking motive.

However, if you do want to branch out from your own interests or expertise, here are some very unscientific, very general guidelines:

Women Seeking Men: Personally, I have noticed the hunkiest men in the home repair or body building sections; the smartest men in the history and cultural studies sections; the "hippest" or "coolest" men in the new fiction section; the most sensitive; "nineties-type" men in the psychology, gardening, poetry, or new age sections; and the strangest, scariest-looking men in the SciFi section.

Men Seeking Women: Bombshells—romance, physical fitness, health, general how-to; smartest—women's studies, cultural studies, science, philosophy; old-fashioned or back-to-nature types—gardening, cooking, yoga; hippest/coolest—new fiction, performing arts, visual arts, erotica.

Same Sex: If you are looking for same sex-partners, remember that 10 percent of almost any section is likely to be gay. However, for a greater concentration of the aforementioned, try performing arts and cooking for gay men; and gay women's fiction, law, physical education, women's health, or gender studies for lesbians. Also, most bookstores have a gay interest section.

By far the best section for mingling with *anyone* is the travel section. It is the most natural thing in the world to compare notes on places you have been or want to go, or get advice on what guide book to take to London or Paris.

Once you have selected your "hunting ground" and staked out your prospect, you then have two choices for the execution of your pickup (please note, these are the same two basic options you have when approaching *any* stranger in *any* social situation).

1. Observation:

   "That looks like an interesting book."

   "Oh I've read that, it's fabulous."

   "I *hate* the way this area is organized."

   "Can you really understand that stuff?"

   "I always get so overwhelmed in here—there are so many books. Maybe they breed after closing."

2. Asking a Question:

   "Excuse me, have you ever read anything by this author? I don't want to waste my money and somehow I think I would trust your opinion."

   "Do you know what kind of gardening book is right for beginners?

   "Would you mind holding this ladder for me?"

   "I know you don't work here, but do you know where I might find _____ [any title with the word sex in it]?"

As for mingling in the bookstore-café, it's more or less the same as mingling in any coffee bar. It's very difficult unless you are forced to take an empty seat at the table of some handsome stranger—which is only acceptable if there are no empty tables left—and then hope the person isn't too absorbed in reading to talk to you. The easiest opening tactic is to ask about what the other person is reading. (If the person is not reading but just staring off into space, comment on the coffee. "Is that a latte or a frappaccino?") However, be sure not to interrupt a reading stranger more than once if your initial gambit inspires no response. A person who is reading may really want to read, and you will be setting yourself up for some brutal rejection if you persist—especially since your only way to escape after such loss of face is to get up and leave.

Dear Miss Mingle:

I was recently at a large party in a nightclub with a date and some other friends. During the evening I was introduced to a very attractive woman, who took me aside at the first opportunity and said, sotto voce, "If you weren't with a date I'd rip your clothes off." I barely managed to smile and answer, "So nice to meet you, too."

My question is this: Should I have managed a wittier immediate reply, and what, if anything, should I have said later on in response to this kind of come-on?

Flabbergasted in Florida

Dear Flabbergasted:

Emily Post would turn over in her grave if she could hear the kinds of things strangers now say to each other. A slight smile and a nod before turning away is all that's required in responding to this kind of shock-loving gal. However, if it should happen again and you feel the need for ready wit:

To encourage her (which is probably not a good idea, but hey, it's your life): "If I weren't with a date, I'd let you."

To discourage (and disarm) her: "Not if I saw you first, ma'am."

Parties and Partners

It's bad enough they leave the car windows down or the toilet seat up, that they don't give you all your telephone messages, and that they invite their mothers over without telling you; you also have to suffer through going to parties with them. The ironic thing is that all your life you wanted someone to go to parties with, and now you often want nothing more than to not have to deal with the annoying way your mate socializes.

Most of the letters I receive from spouses with mingling questions present problems that could be pretty well fixed by the partners' communicating with each other better (*Hello?* Has anyone ever heard of couples therapy?) and are merely symptoms of larger relationship issues. However, in my responses I have tried as much as possible to stay out of the marital war zone and limit myself to the banter-filled battlefield of mingling.

Dear Miss Mingle:

What can I do when I am at a social gathering and my husband starts telling things about me that I do not particularly want aired in public? I have told him not to do this but he gets carried away; I guess he forgets. He seems to think it is amusing.

Blushing Bride

Dear Blushing Bride:

You could always try using the old dog trainers' method, which believe it or not often works surprisingly well on men. This method consists of simple and immediate punishment or reward. In other words, when your husband begins to share your secrets with his buddies, if you are close enough to him, quickly step on his toe, pinch him hard, or spill something on him. If he gets the message and changes the subject right away, you then reward him with a plate of hors d'oeuvres. As with canines, this negative-positive reinforcement *must be given at the moment the bad deed is done;* talking to your husband about it later is useless, as you well know.

Another fun way to change your husband's tune pretty fast is to fight fire with fire. As soon as your loose-lipped louse of a spouse begins hauling out your dirty laundry, start sharing things that will embarrass *him.* Talk about the cute little mewing noise he makes when sleeping, or about how he loves to paint your toenails. Or embarrass him in other ways: Do your Jimmy Durante or Ronald Reagan imitation in front of his boss—whatever you think will humiliate him the most. Then, when he takes you aside and in a terrified whisper asks you what the heck you think you're doing, tell him sweetly but firmly that this is what he can expect every time he tells stories about you that he shouldn't be telling.

If this doesn't work, consider hypnosis, shock treatments, or obedience school.

Dear Miss Mingle:

I am at my wit's end. Whenever my girlfriend and I are at a party or out with friends, she interrupts me constantly. I know I should talk to her about this, but we haven't been going out all that long and I don't feel I can get into it without hurting her feelings. She doesn't do this when we are alone (or I wouldn't still be with her). Is there something I can do to make her stop it? I'm about to lose it.

Cut-Off in Connecticut

Dear Cut-Off:

People who interrupt a lot are probably insecure. Perhaps when your girlfriend becomes more confident in the relationship she will stop this irritating habit. You really shouldn't let it go on too long, however. You've no idea how painful the behavior is for people around you, not to mention the fact that you may crack at any moment and pour a bowl of hot soup over her head.

If you really feel you can't talk to her about the problem (and I must emphasize that telling her how you feel *is* by far the best way to go) you might try repeatedly interrupting *her* interruptions with a pointed, "As I was *saying...*" or "So *anyway...*" and see if she gets the message. It probably won't work though. In general, interrupt-itis is a hard disease to cure.

Dear Miss Mingle:

My husband has many friends, some of whose wives I know only slightly. Often when a couple comes to visit, the men carry on a conversation with each other, and I, of course, am expected to talk to the wife. One wife in particular is very boring and constantly discourses on things that are of no interest to me. It drives me crazy. I would prefer if we could all join in together but am at a loss as to how to make it happen.

Bored to Tears

Dear Bored to Tears:

I have no choice but to assume that there is a reason you are willing to put up with this unpleasant arrangement in the first place. Perhaps you owe your husband big-time because he suffers through decorator's shows with you or you force him to sit through *The Sound of Music* on a regular basis. I also must assume that your husband knows how you feel, but still expects you to divert the boring wife while he has a good time with the husband. If this is the case you have two choices: 1) You can figure out how to survive the conversation with this femme banal; or 2) You can defy your husband's old-fashioned, cigar-and-brandy-in-the-den preference for male bonding and find a way to merge the men's and women's conversations.

In the first case, you might try one of the following How to Survive Conversing with Truly Boring People methods:

1. Drink heavily (not recommended for borderline alcoholics or people who have to drive anywhere).

2. Give her a taste of her own medicine: Be more boring than she is. Talk about yourself incessantly, recite recipes, tell your life story, list your children's countless accomplishments.

3. Feed her. Constantly. So that her mouth is full most of the time.

4. If there is another woman (or women) present besides Ms. Monotonous, join forces with this other woman to overpower Ms. M. and wrest control of the conversation. The best way to do this is for you and this other woman to ask each other direct and personal questions as constantly as possible. Interrupt Madame Boring if you have to, even though you were taught it isn't polite. (Hey, we're talking survival here.)

5. Learn how to sleep with your eyes open.

In the second case—that is, if uniting the men and the women is your goal—congratulations. You've entered the twentieth century. There are several different methods you can employ to successfully meld the males and females.

A lot of people use the Let's Ask the Men method. Here's how it's done: Try to wait until an appropriate subject comes up in your conversation with Mrs. Yawn and then make an enthusiastic pretense of having to get your husband's (or even *her* husband's) opinion on the subject. It doesn't necessarily have to be a traditionally "male" topic; it can be something about your children ("Darling, when did little Johnny lose his first tooth?"), something about a mutual friend ("Isn't Sam Hill having his house painted?"), something about the universe ("Hey, Joe, what *is* a black hole, anyway?"), anything—just make sure it's something that's not *exclusively* female. If the men are in the same room as the women, and fairly nearby, you need only shift your body position slightly as you put the query to your husband. Make sure, however, that you do more than just look over your shoulder. Your body language must clearly indicate that you (and your Duchess of Dull, of course) are now officially engaged in a conversation with the men. If, on the other hand, the men are in another room—or are in the same room but far away— you are going to need to excuse yourself as follows: "Hold on, I want to ask Charlie what he thinks. I'll be right back." Then, when you get to the men, you ask your question, then say, "Come on back and join us, we're getting lonely for you." A warning squeeze somewhere on your husband's person sometimes helps at this point.

(Please note: You *will* have to blatantly interrupt the men's conversation, but that's okay. All's fair in love and boredom.)

Another effective ploy for herding in wayward husbands is a time-honored one: food. Put out some mouth-watering food—preferably a messy dip that needs to be eaten in the vicinity of the serving bowl (and don't put out plates that the men can take back to their men-only corner)—and then sit back and watch the guys miraculously wander back to you. (This may sound sexist, but it's not. If the men wanted the women to talk to *them* and *they* put out tempting food, it would bring the women running just as fast. Especially if it were chocolate.)

If neither of these two techniques works, you may have to resort to more desperate (and old-fashioned) measures: have an accident, see a mouse, find something that needs lifting, play a party game, or start taking your clothes off.

P.S. This situation hardly ever happens in reverse; that is, that the man gets stuck with a boring husband. The reason is twofold: for one thing women are so much better socialized that they usually won't leave their husbands in this situation, and for another, when men are bored, they just talk sports and they're fine.

Dear Miss Mingle:

My wife is a what some people would call a knockout. I'm not complaining, but when we go to parties the men are all over her. How can I subtly let people at a party know that she is attached to me—without coming off like a Neanderthal?

Possessive in Poughkeepsie

Dear Possessive:

It's completely your wife's prerogative how, when, and whether or not to let other men know she's "taken." Furthermore, if she's *that* beautiful, the fact that she's married is not going to keep the real wolves away. Let her have a good time and you try to do the same. Console yourself with the fact that it's you she married, after all.

However, if at any time she should indicate that she needs and wants your protection or interference (many couples have secret signals for just this kind of thing), then, by all means, put on your shining armor and get over there. Put your arm around her and say something like, "Is my wife giving you any trouble over here?" (*never*, "Is this man bothering you?") and then as soon as you can, tell the aggressor(s) that you have to borrow your wife from them because somebody on the other side of the room wants to meet her.

Dear Miss Mingle:

My husband always disappears at parties. He often doesn't talk to anyone, and many times I will find him hiding in another room by himself, reading a book. He says he is not unhappy, but my evening is partly ruined with worrying about him. He does this vanishing act even when we give a party! And then I have to run the party all by myself. Help!

Together but Separate

Dear Together but Separate:

Your husband sounds like a classic minglephobic. These kinds of hard-core loners are difficult nuts to crack, but you can try one of the following Remedies for Extreme Minglephobia:

Employment: Give the minglephobic a job to do. Get him to pass food, hang coats, pour drinks. Make sure you keep him busy with tasks that necessitate his interacting with people.

Matchmaking: Arrange a "minglephobics' corner" at the party. Sit your minglephobic down with another proven minglephobic or someone who looks like he may be one. The idea is to find someone *else* who is repelled by the idea of mingling with a lot of people, someone who would therefore happily commit to a long sit-down conversation in a quiet niche, out of the fray. By matching your hermit-like husband up with a kindred spirit, you ensure that he is—at least in a small way—participating in the party. It may not be the ideal situation, but it's certainly better than his being all alone in another room reading Proust.

Shepherding: This is a beefed-up version of what you probably already do; that is, to intermittently go find your husband and herd him back into the party. What will help, however, is to have other shepherds to aid you so that you don't have to personally check up on him every twenty minutes. Entreat one or two friends to alternate with you in seeking out your minglephobic and firmly guiding him back to the main room under the guise of his being introduced to someone. Believe it or not, if the minglephobic is continually driven back to the party, he will eventually learn that his solitude is an impossibility. You may even find him inexplicably returning to the party all on his own.

Dear Miss Mingle:

My wife is very shy. A lab researcher by trade, she isn't used to making small talk; whereas I am in public relations and am at ease in almost any social situation. When we go to parties she sticks to me like glue and I feel like I have a shadow I can't shake off. I can't help wishing she would go do her own mingling. On the other hand, I would feel terrible if she ended up standing by herself in the corner. Can you give me any advice?

Joined at the Hip

Dear Joined at the Hip:

The best technique for helping out a shy partner or friend, which will at the same time allow you some mingling space, is something I call Conversational Procurement. It may sound a bit complicated but will be well worth mastering given your partner's party proclivities. Basically the idea is to lead as many people as you can—like sacrificial lambs—to your wallflower of a wife. Figuratively speaking, what you are going to do is hand-feed her a virtual feast of conversational partners. Just follow these step-by-step instructions:

Step one: Upon entering the party scene, first guide your shrinking violet to someone you both know. (Let's call this hypothetical person Mack.) Try to get your wife involved in the conversation right away using common conversational ploys such as, "My wife feels exactly the same way, don't you, honey?" "Mack, you must tell my wife about the time you..." or "Get my wife to explain that; she's the only one I know who understands it!" Always be as complimentary to her as you can without embarrassing her, to help build up her confidence.

Step two: While your wife or Mack is in the middle of a thought, excuse yourself for a brief period of time. Go and get drinks or food for yourself and your wife, put your coats in the other room or go on some other errand. This will be your wife's trial separation. Make sure you *do* return to her in five minutes or so with the promised drink or food for her. She must feel from the start that you are watching out for her and that you will never leave her alone for very long.

Step three: If your wife and Mack are miraculously still involved in a lively conversation by the time you get back, give your wife an encouraging signal in the way of some kind of physical gesture (a slight squeeze of her shoulders, a hand on her waist) and say, "Excuse me honey, excuse me Mack, I've got to say hello to _____, but I'll be right back." You then leave her with the accommodating Mack for the time being. If, on the other hand, Mack has escaped from your wife before you can return with the drinks, you then collect your Timid Tillie, take her over to another person or group, get the conversation going as before, then leave her there.

Step four: From this point on, you will be bringing people over to your wife. Here's how it's done:

Let's say you have been talking to a man for about ten minutes, and the conversation has taken an uninteresting turn—perhaps he is regaling you about the intricacies of the new tax code. Wait for him to take a breath, then say, "I'm sorry but my wife has *got* to hear this. She was just asking me about this the other night." Take him by the arm and physically lead him to your wife. Introduce them, and you're off again with a casual "Be right back." (This is technically not a lie as you *will* be back, again and again, delivering your mate a constant stream of people with whom to converse.) This sly maneuver is actually a dual-purpose variation of a commonly-employed exit technique known as the Human Sacrifice. You use your wife to help you get out of your current conversation—so that you are free to mingle with someone else—and at the same time you use your former conversational partner to keep your minglephobic wife happily occupied.

Please note: Don't wait for an undesirable conversation to offer an acquaintance up to your wife. After having ten to fifteen minutes of conversation with any one person—even if it's the most fascinating person in the room—you should escort him or her over to your wife. If your clinging bride is left alone for more than a minute she will be at your side once again, and you will have to begin the process all over.

Dear Miss Mingle:

I am an art dealer and both attend and host many business gatherings. I mingle like a maniac (and probably make a fool of myself in the process) at social events and parties. My partner in the art gallery, on the other hand, doesn't even bother to try: She zeroes in on one person and talks intensely with him or her as long as she can, often holing up in a corner and giving no indication that she notices anyone else in the room. Several times I've been left to face the crowd all by myself, with my supposed "partner" safely squirreled away having a tête-à-tête.

After the last opening we attended together, I confronted her with this problem. She claimed that she was merely giving special attention to the man she was concentrating on—who was, in fact, an important client-

prospect *we'd often dreamed of snagging. However, this was not an isolated incident; she does this all the time (sometimes with a personal friend while there are clients left for me to schmooze alone). In short, she's a total non-mingler. When looking for her in any crowded room, I always find her motionless in a corner, as if she had glue on the soles of her shoes.*

How can I make her see what she's doing? Should I abandon mingling myself? Should I beat her to the punch at our next party and start a one-on-one conversation with someone before she has a chance? It seems so rude.

Left Holding the Mingle Bag

Dear Left Holding:

Two wrongs don't make a right. Good grief, what would happen to your business if you both threw in the mingling towel? As for your uncooperative comrade, I know it's hard to hear this, but I have learned over the years that what comes easy to some of us is terrifying to many. Your partner may be hiding a deep-seated minglephobia.

You might try bringing people over to meet her—wherever she is—at the next affair. Since she is your business partner, it should be perfectly acceptable to interrupt her with a light-hearted, "Excuse me, I knew you would want to meet Mr._____," or "Mr. _____, you must meet my wonderful partner." You can also continually send people to your partner: "See that woman over there? In the green dress? That's my partner, Mitzy Smith. She told me she really wanted to meet you." A somewhat nastier, but nonetheless effective trick is for you to steal the object of your partner's tête-à-tête away from her: "Oh, there you are, Mr. _____! Excuse me, I must borrow him, Mitzy; someone is dying to meet him."

Ideally, if you could somehow reconcile yourself to your partner's nonmingling mingle style, and she could admit that this is indeed her modus operandi, you might benefit by holding a Pre-Party Strategy Session. These can be very constructive for business functions. For instance, you and your partner could *both* decide which important contact should be her main focus for the evening and at the same time decide what your own goals should be. Help and encourage each other in what you each do best. Halfway through the party, check in with each other to see how it's going and to see if there is someone else present who isn't being sufficiently schmoozed because you are stretched too thin. At that point, perhaps your partner will agree for the good of the business to at least switch to a *different* one-on-one conversation.

If none of this works, maybe you should pull a no-show at the next affair. Perhaps your partner would learn to fly if she knew she was the only one at the controls.

Dear Miss Mingle:

My wife has this terrible habit at parties. After she has about two drinks she will start to sing at the top of her lungs. Our friends and acquaintances know she will perform in this manner on request, and request they do (<u>they</u> think it's a riot). It wouldn't be so bad, but she loves to imitate Barbra Streisand. I am beyond embarrassed on these occasions. How can I keep this from happening?

Totally Mortified

Dear Totally Mortified:

So what's wrong with a little singing? Your wife's having a good time, everyone else is having a good time—where is the problem? The world needs more people singing at the top of their lungs—not fewer—and that goes for singing while mingling, too.

****

Miss Mingle's Rules for Partners

1. Don't mingle as a pair. You see each other enough and won't meet as many people staying together. Split up, even if you come back to each other intermittently to recharge.

2. Help each other out. Warn your partner about clusters of deadly bores or the occasional drunk so he or she doesn't have to go through what you just did.

3. Don't tell personal things about your partner at the party—even if they make great stories—unless you are sure you have his or her permission.

4. Don't make plans or commit the two of you socially while you are at a party and, by so doing, put your partner on the spot ("Doesn't that sound good, honey?"). Get into the habit of saying "We'll have to go home and check our schedules."

5. Don't hang all over your partner in public. Beyond the seventh grade, public displays of affection are definitely out.

****

Help for the Hopeless Host

Right before I'm about to give a party I usually get a terrible, sick feeling in my stomach. This sensation of nausea is not caused by sampling too much dip. It is not caused by over-excitement at the prospect of seeing a potential beau or a celebrity guest. No, this is the uneasy feeling that is born solely of the mortifying memories of parties past.

There was that horrible time I muffed the invitations and managed to invite both the current and the ex-girlfriend of my friend Paul (the ex-girlfriend drank too much gin and wouldn't leave). Then there was the time I prepared for a cocktail party for fifty and only eleven showed up—that included the neighbor who I snared at the last minute to try to fill the room. And, of course,

I'll never forget the party during which one of my guests (a would-be writer) kept going up to everyone else there and saying, "Do *you* want to be my agent?"

When you decide to host any kind of party, you are really asking for it. But if you're like me, you'll risk just about anything for the wonderful energy you get (not the anxiety, but that *other* feeling) from having a collection of friends gathered together in your home. And no matter what else happens, I always try to emulate the famous hostess Elsa Maxwell, who, with only three words, always made sure her guests felt welcome: "When they arrive," she is quoted as saying, "I murmur, 'at last,' and when they arise to depart I protest, 'already?'"

Dear Miss Mingle:

Often when I am entertaining dinner guests at home, I excuse myself to prepare food in the kitchen. Invariably someone will follow me in and keep talking to me while I am working. I find it very hard to concentrate on what I am doing and yet I don't want to be rude to the person. Help!

Frazzled Hostess

Dear Frazzled:

You can always be candid and say, "I'm sorry to admit this, but I never have been able to cook and talk at the same time. It's a type of dyslexia, I'm afraid. Would you care to help me with this?" Or "Stop! Your story is so interesting I can't remember how many cloves of garlic I used!" However, as a lover of intrigue, I much prefer the following sneakier tactics:

• Get a trusted friend or partner to be on the lookout for kitchen raiders of this sort. Your comrade's job will be to follow the distracting person into the kitchen and distract *her* by engaging her in conversation, while you continue cooking in peace.

• Even more cheeky (and potentially more effective) is to have various items ready in the kitchen—items that desperately need to be carried somewhere else. Then, when that pesty guest starts talking to you while you are trying to sauté the scallops, simply interrupt politely with a "Would you mind terribly if I asked you to take this _____ out to the table?" Please note: Try to have a lot of (preferably complicated) fetch-and-carry tasks lined up. You may need to send the guest on this type of mission several times before she either gets the message or gets tired of helping.

Dear Miss Mingle:

I am a single woman who moved to New York several months ago. Last week, after I came home from a party, I mentioned to my roommate that I didn't feel like I'd met very many people at the party. My roommate said, "Didn't the hostess introduce you to anyone?" I realized that she hadn't. Miss Mingle, I grew up in the South where a gracious hostess would have seen to it that people were properly introduced. In this more casual, modern age, how can I get the hostess to introduce me—particularly to single men—without seeming pushy, and without letting the single men know I wanted to be introduced? I love New York, but how can I adapt to these Yankees' lack of good manners?

Missing Mississippi

Dear Missing Mississippi:

I hate to tell you this, but if you moved to New York looking for good manners you are pretty much out of luck. However, I happen to believe this particular laziness on the part of hosts is more generational than geographical. I don't quite know how we lost the art of being good hosts, but I believe (at the risk of sounding like my grandmother) it has something to do with rock and roll. (If it's too loud for introductions, why bother?)

Unfortunately, the best way to deal with this problem is not a subtle one and may not appeal to your Southern sensibilities. Nonetheless, what you should do is take the hostess aside and ask her very nicely if she would mind introducing you to some of the people you don't know. This not only takes care of your own needs, but also serves to gently instruct the hostess as to what her hostly duties are. But be very sure you *don't* tell her to introduce you to single men, unless you can really trust her not to—after a few martinis—pave your way with a light-hearted, "Darling Mary here wants to meet single men—are you still single, Bobby-Baby?" In any case, it is usually much less daunting to meet a single man indirectly: that is, you meet him because you are talking to a friend of his and he joins in, or you meet him and several other people at the same time.

Your other option for getting introduced at a party is to become your own hostess. Imagine the real hostess has been called away on urgent matters and everyone is pitching in and taking over for her. Approach people with, "I don't believe we've met yet, I'm _____" or "Betty hasn't had a chance to introduce us. I'm _____." I have always found this direct approach to be very effective. However, if you really insist on going Southern, you can always play Damsel in Distress and ask another *guest* to introduce you around. ("I just don't know a soul, here, I'm afraid I'll just be a little ol' wall flower!")

One last note: If this party you speak of was in New York City, there is an extremely good chance that there *were* no single men there—not straight ones anyway. You might think about moving. (I think about it all the time.)

Dear Miss Mingle:

I am sick and tired of the nineties. The other night I gave a dinner party for ten. I had slaved for hours to make a fabulous five-course meal. When one of my guests arrived (the date of a male friend), she peeked into the kitchen and announced that she was sorry but she couldn't eat any of the things I had prepared— except for the green salad. She was a strict vegetarian—she didn't eat fish, meat, or dairy products—and on top of that she was "allergic" to yeast, so she couldn't have bread or wine. The rest of the guests and I felt guilty throughout the meal, and it dampened the spirits of all present to have one guest picking at a plate of salad while the rest of us gorged on various politically incorrect dishes.

I guess I should have prepared for such a contingency, but shouldn't her date have let me know beforehand of her strict eating requirements? What could I have done to make the incident less of a downer for everybody else?

Hostile Hostess

Dear Hostile Hostess:

While it is true that in many social circles it is not unlikely that one out of ten people will be a vegetarian, there is still ABSOLUTELY NO excuse for someone showing up at a dinner party without having somehow let the hostess know about such all-encompassing requirements or aversions. Furthermore, any guest who *does* show up with these requirements should make every effort to help those enjoying the forbidden foods to feel comfortable.

If this ever happens again, I would suggest the following:

Don't apologize for not having the right food for the vegetarian. You had no way of knowing her preferences; it is not your problem. Politely suggest to your friend that he might want to go out and get some food his date can eat or order takeout. (Make sure he knows you are not going to pay, however. "This place is very good but I don't know how much you want to spend," should do the trick.) In any case, *don't* let the vegetarian eat all the salad. You can say something like "Gee, if I'd have known, I would have made more salad," indicating that you must reserve some for other guests. *Don't* try to pretend there's nothing awkward going on. During the meal, encourage the rest of the party to give the vegetarian a little good-natured teasing ("You sure you don't want some of this delicious venison?") and, if your guests seem interested, lead them in a lively discussion of vegetarianism, or macrobiotic diets. Then move on to something else. The idea is to dwell on it just enough to give your other guests permission to enjoy their meal, and to remind everyone that the responsibility for the situation belongs entirely with the yeast-allergic vegetarian.

P.S. If your male friend does not call within forty-eight hours to apologize, cross him off your dinner guest list.

Dear Miss Mingle:

Some time ago an artist friend of mine gave me a very abstract, modern painting that she had painted. At the time she gave it to me, she and I had a lengthy conversation about the work, during which she explained to me the underlying philosophy of the aesthetics, why the painting is what it is, etc. Now, a couple of years later, after moving to another house where I finally have a big enough space to hang the painting, I can't remember which way is up—and nobody I show the painting to can figure it out either. I am expecting the artist to come to a party at my house next week and I fear I may offend her— what if it's hung wrong? Should I say anything?

Panic Stricken

Dear Panic Stricken:

You definitely have a problem. It's too bad your friend didn't sign the painting. (I think a lot of modern artists sign their works on the back just so you can tell which is the top and the bottom.)

I hate to disappoint you, but unless you can get a psychic to solve this puzzle for you, you really only have two options—neither one of which is going to sound too appealing. The first course of action is to tell the truth. When the friend comes to your house, take her aside quietly and say something like, "I know I'm a stupid idiot, and I really do love the painting you gave me, and I know we had a conversation about it, but I am afraid I may not have hung it quite right." Don't say *specifically* that you think you may have hung it upside down, as there is always the chance that it is right side up, in which case your friend will, hopefully, think you are merely referring to how you've framed it, or how you've arranged it on the wall.

Your other option is probably the one most people would choose, but it may result in the matter haunting you forever. That is to say nothing at all about it. If the painting *is* hung incorrectly, your friend may not be that offended. After all, if her work is abstract, she is more than likely used to this kind of thing. (I bet you are not the first one of her friends to find themselves in this very quandary.) She will probably say nothing about it, or tell you quite offhandedly that you may want to try turning the thing around.

However, if you say nothing about it and your friend informs you that the painting is hung upside down—and you can see she is offended—you can try to get yourself off the hook with one of the following lines. But frankly, Miss Mingle wouldn't want to be in your shoes:

"I *knew* that was the wrong way! My ex-wife [ex-husband/decorator/roommate/etc.] *insisted* that was right. She wouldn't listen to me."

"Well, what the...? Good Lord, the maid [my husband/the carpenter] must have taken that down and hung it back up the wrong way!" (Acting annoyed, take the painting off the wall and hang it back up the other way.)

Laugh loudly and call to your spouse: "She noticed it right away, honey! You owe me five bucks!"

Dear Miss Mingle:

I recently had a totally nightmarish experience at a party I threw. It wasn't until most of the guests had arrived that I realized that two of the girls I invited were both under the impression that they were there as my "date." Sally, who I have been going with for several months, arrived first. Fifteen minutes later, the doorbell rang and it was Gina, this girl I had recently gone out with a couple times. (I had mentioned the party to Gina only after she had told me she was going to be out of town.) Neither girl knew anything about the other one.

I was really sweating it through the whole party, as both Sally and Gina kept sort of making proprietary moves on me, like putting their arms around my waist, etc., and both of them made it clear they were going to stay until the party was over. As the evening wore on, my prospects for survival looked bleaker and bleaker, until, finally, there we were, just Sally, Gina, and me. I didn't know what to do, so I opened another bottle of wine for the three of us. (It was red wine, but it was certainly served with a chill.) Finally both of them figured out what was going on, and they both left pretty steamed.

I know this shouldn't have happened in the first place, but after both girls showed up, is there anything I could have done to make the situation better?

Crashed and Burned

Dear Crashed and Burned:

Your letter made my head whirl. If you think *you* had it bad, imagine how the two women felt. But I am not here to lecture you, as I am *sure* you have learned all about playing two ends against the middle.

The only way to have salvaged such a disastrous

evening would have been to salvage *half* of it. In other words, you should have made it clear right away which one of your girlfriends you meant to be your date. I assume that would have been Sally; but, in any case, the correct behavior is to be very polite to the extra woman while at the same time indicating in no uncertain terms your relationship with the primary one—by putting your arm around the favored female, asking her in a familiar way to help you in the kitchen, or publicly announcing your plans for brunch the next day. Then at least only one woman would be hurt, not to mention the fact that you would stand a small chance of holding on to the other one, instead of ending up alone.

Though I have a sneaking suspicion a guy like you wouldn't be alone for long.

Dear Miss Mingle:

What do you do about guests who won't go home when the party is over? Every time we have people over to our house it's the same story. I guess people don't have to get up as early as my husband and I do (or maybe our parties are too much fun!), but somehow there is always one guest who has comfortably settled in and won't stop talking. We've tried yawning and making comments about how early we have to get up the next day, but it doesn't seem to do much good. We don't want to hurt the guest's feelings. I hope you can help us. The older we get the less patience we have for this problem.

Bleary-Eyed in Bloomington

Dear Bleary-Eyed:

I've always felt that someone should make a horror movie called *The Guest Who Wouldn't Leave*. It certainly can be an agonizing experience when all you want to do is tidy up and go to bed, and that last hanger-on refills his glass, puts his feet up on your coffee table, and begins telling you in great detail about his childhood in Iowa.

While I must confess I hardly ever have this particular problem (I'm usually sad when guests leave, no matter what time it is), here are a few tricks I know for shaking off that late-staying guest:

Clean-Up: Start clearing away dirty dishes and glasses, empty ashtrays, etc. Keep talking to the guest while you are doing this (you don't want to be *too* rude), but don't ask the guest any questions or encourage him to elaborate. If there are two of you hosting, *both* of you must begin cleaning up to get your point across. The guest will be forced to follow you around the house as you work, which should get his blood moving enough for him to realize he's overstayed his welcome. And the minute he says anything remotely like, "I guess I should probably get going soon," quickly respond with, "Well, ordinarily we'd *love* to have you stay longer, but I have an early meeting tomorrow. Do you need a cab?"

Run Out of Refreshments: The success of this ploy depends on the guest and on how well you can hide the leftovers. After you become aware you have a problem guest, stop offering the guest anything to eat or drink. If the thick-headed guest *asks* for another drink, smile apologetically and say, "I'm so sorry but we seem to have run out of just about everything. Can I get you a glass of water?" If he is uncouth enough to request more food, respond in a similar fashion.

Play Good Host, Bad Host: This ruse is for couples only. Decide who's going to be the good host and who's going to be the bad host. When it gets to the point that you can't stand it anymore and are beginning to think the person will never leave, whoever is playing the bad host should yawn, stand up, and excuse himself with, "I'm afraid I've got to hit the hay. I'm dead on my feet. Goodnight, Mr. _____. Don't forget to put the garbage out, sweetheart." After the bad host has disappeared, the good host then apologizes for the bad host, while emphasizing how much it *is* past his bedtime. Even a total dunderhead should get the message and pack it in.

Abandon ship: One sure way to get a guest out the door is to get out the door yourself. Use this strategy when your party is in the middle of the day or in the early evening and you therefore can't use your bedtime as an excuse. What you do is to plan to have somewhere else to go about an hour after the official ending time of the party. For example, if your shower invitation says: 11:00–2:00 (and your invitation should *always* have an ending time or you are asking for trouble), have somewhere you must be at 3:00. That way, at about 2:45 you can say you're sorry but you promised to take your mother to the grocery store, you have a meeting at your kid's school, or you promised to drop off something somewhere. If in actuality you don't have any place to go, you may have to walk out the door anyway to get the person to leave.

On the other hand, if it's *not* the middle of the night, maybe you won't mind a slow-to-leave guest or two. They can help you clean up and you can gossip about everyone else.

P.S. Once in a while you can end up with someone in your house who *really* won't leave, no matter what you do. (Usually these extreme types are either drunk or emotionally disturbed.) In this case, you may be forced to use the Last Resort Method for Expelling a Guest: Send him out for beer. Then lock the door, turn off the lights, and don't answer the bell.

Dear Miss Mingle:

What are you supposed to do when two people who have come to a party at your house get into a very loud argument? This happened to me the other night and it really destroyed the evening. One of them inadvertently insulted the other and nothing the rest of us could do or say would stop the fight. The party came to a screeching halt.

Reluctant Referee

Dear Reluctant Referee:

This is very unfortunate situation for all involved and is one of the things that can kill a party—fast. Although a few of your more puerile guests may see such a mid-party scene as entertainment, most will find it embarrassing or disturbing. It is extremely bad form for people to lose control like that in someone else's home, but it does happen occasionally. There are two recommended methods for dealing with angry party guests:

Method 1: Separate and Divert. The first thing to do—as with ill-behaved children—is to try to separate them. Your objective is to do this with as little drama as possible. Immediately go over to the troublesome twosome and, smiling, take one of them by the arm and firmly pull her in the direction of another room, or to a distant part of the same room. If you can enlist someone to collect the other angry guest at the same time, and pull her in the opposite direction, so much the better. Then stay with your boiled-over guest until you can get her involved in another conversation. Keep an eye on both of them during the rest of the party to see that they don't end up together again. *Never* take sides in the argument—at least not during the party—and try not to let either irascible guest drink any more alcohol.

Method 2: Social surgery. This course of action is usually taken when Method 1 has failed; that is, the two people fighting refuse to be separated. Just as a doctor would try to isolate a virus or cut out a tumor so the rest of the body can remain healthy, you must endeavor to remove the offensive pair from the rest of the guests. Where to move them depends on how violent the argument is. If it has become physical—or verbally abusive to the point that it's scary—you should escort

the perpetrator or perpetrators of the violence immediately out of your house or apartment, with the help of
a few of your stronger guests. (Never forget it's *your*
home.) If you don't feel there's a danger of anyone
coming to blows or breaking anything, and you want to
cause less of a scene, push the two altercators into
another room with a "Maybe you guys could work this
out in private," and close the door. Or, if the party is
small enough, you can gather up the well-behaved
guests and move *them* somewhere else, leaving the bad-
behaved guests to duke it out where they are.

Method 3: Guest Dousing. Pouring cold water on the
out-of-control guests is not an entirely bad idea. It was
done in old movies to great effect. However, this
method is not recommended, as it tends to ruin your
furniture.

Restarting the Party: A party is like a living orga-
nism, and after such a wound, some healing must
occur. Guests may be so stunned at the outburst they've
witnessed that they are at best momentarily derailed
from their own conversations and at worst wondering
how long it will take them to get the hell out of there.
After you have dealt with the offensive guests, there
will be a critical period of awkward silence during
which it is your job as host to jump-start the party. It is
usually best not to try to pretend nothing unusual has
occurred, but to instead use a humorous comment to
get the party going again. The line should be delivered
to the group at large, and will serve to release the
tension as well as to cause the remaining guests to

bond, like people who have survived an earthquake together.

Some party jump-start lines are:

"Okay, who put the truth serum in the punch?"

"Is there a therapist in the house?"

"Well, I couldn't get a musician so I'm afraid *that* will have to suffice for entertainment."

"Can I throw a party or can I throw a party!"

"Okay, folks—drinks are on the house!"

****

Dealing With Deadly Party Pauses

At small parties there may be one or two terrible moments—for whatever reason—when everyone stops talking at once. Don't panic—emergency help is at hand:

What a Host Can Do:

• Turn up the music (just a little, don't blast people or make it impossible to talk) so that the silence is less noticeable. And make sure your music doesn't run out while you are too far away to reach it quickly. If possible, have a music control lieutenant to cover for you when you are in the loo.

• Make a toast. About anything—the season, the weather, the party, a guest—it will get people past the feeling that everything has frozen.

• Offer something. Asking guests if they need

anything is a good ploy because *somebody* is bound to want *something*, and then you can move about getting it for them while other people shake themselves out of their temporary stupor.

What a Host Can Say:

• (If guests are eating) "I guess this silence means the food is a success."

• "Is everybody meditating?"

• "Well, I guess you all are waiting for me [for Johnny] to tell my [his] favorite joke."

• "Hmmm...I wonder if this quiet means everyone is at a loss for words or just incredibly relaxed."

• "Are we waiting for the world to end or what?"

****

Dear Miss Mingle:

Last summer I decided to give a party even though I think I am the world's worst host. I swear, my parties are worse than Mary Tyler Moore's ever were. But I figured, what the hey, I have got to pay back all the people who have invited me to their parties for the last two years.

Everything was copacetic until this one wacky chick (who I don't know too well) began yelling, "Let's play charades! Let's play charades!" She then proceeded to organize everybody she could into playing. Most people looked like deer caught in the headlights of an oncoming

car—including me. I didn't know what to do. I know that
the majority of the people there definitely did not want to
play charades. How do I know this? Because they all left
shortly after the game began.

Miss Mingle, please tell me how I could have kept this
from happening.

Milquetoast Host

Dear Milquetoast Host:

Parties are like living entities. They must be allowed
to go their own way, to be what they are going to be, to
follow their own unique paths. As with children, it can
be painful to watch them heading in the wrong direction, but there is sometimes little you can do. And at
the risk of offending, I have to say that if your party was
susceptible to a charades attack, it must have been
pretty weak in the first place.

In general, party games are not a good idea unless
the game is specified beforehand, or unless you have a
small group, all of whom want to play. In the case of the
siege by the charade-crazed woman, you might have
made an effort to take some kind of vote among your
guests to see how many people really wanted to play
charades. In other words, you invoke the democratic
process to prevent the coup. Of course, even if the vote
is ten to one against the game, it may not deter a person
who is bent on charades (they are usually fanatics), but
what it *will* do is to give your guests the feeling of
solidarity necessary for them to resist the takeover.

Or you could just get tough: Say "I'm sorry, I don't allow charades in my home. It's against my religion."

Dear Miss Mingle:

I have a party question about logistics. I like to throw big cocktail parties (my party ideal is the wild party in "Breakfast at Tiffany's"). I have a fairly large apartment. The trouble is, when people first start to arrive, there is so much room that people feel uncomfortable standing, so they sit down in little groups. Then it's hard to get them to stand up again. One time people started moving the furniture, and I ended up with this huge circle of chairs in the middle of the room, which made mingling impossible. Besides ordering everybody to get up, I didn't know what to do! It was horrible.

How can I create the kind of party I want and yet not come off as a militant hostess?

Hostess Without the Mostest

Dear Hostess Without the Mostest:

Your question definitely comes under the heading of advanced mingling. It's very difficult for a hostess to make people do what she wants them to do. No matter what you have envisioned, sometimes people *will* wander off in twos or threes and you'll find them on the balcony, in the kitchen, even in the bathroom, having quiet intimate talks instead of mingling the way you think they should. And, except for arranging the food and drink so that it's in a central location—and not reachable by anyone in chairs or sofas—there isn't much you can do about it. You can try to keep herding everyone back into the living room. However, as with sheep, while you are getting three or four corralled, two more will inevitably escape.

One way to get your guests up on their feet and make them stay on their feet—without ordering them to stand (which you simply can*not* do)—is to call to them from across the room to come and meet so-and so, or to come and help you with moving or carrying this or that. (There is always the "Come taste this dip!" ploy.) A favorite gimmick of mine is to take the first batch of guests on a tour of my apartment or show them something new I've acquired. This sometimes keeps them standing long enough for the masses to begin to arrive. But the only *surefire* way to make sure people all mingle together, standing up, is to have very few chairs available and shut off the other rooms.

As for your fantasy of recreating Holly Golightly's wild bash, forget it. I've tried for years (I've got the cigarette holder to prove it). Alas, without Audrey Hepburn it simply doesn't work.

Dear Miss Mingle:

I want to know what a host can do when someone turns on the television during his party. I was so flabbergasted when this happened during a buffet dinner I was giving last fall, I didn't know what to do. I was in the other room getting somebody a drink, and when I returned, the TV was on. Okay, it was the National League playoffs, but still.

I feel as if it really disrupted the party. Even though many of the guests seemed to be enjoying the game, shouldn't they have stayed home if they wanted to see it?

Out of (Remote) Control

Dear Out of (Remote) Control:

Let's be absolutely clear on one thing. Television is a drug. A powerful one. To turn on a TV in a room full of people is like handing around syringes filled with heroin. Just observe any group of people if there is a TV on in the room; they cannot *not* watch it. It is the absolute death knell of any social gathering, unless the express purpose of the gathering was to watch TV.

In this, the Age of Television, I know a lot of people will disagree with me, but *under no circumstances* does any guest have the right to turn your party into a TV-viewing event. Even if he were to have been discreet enough to go into another room to watch (assuming you have TVs in more than one room, as almost every American does), it is still totally unacceptable. Even if it is Superbowl Sunday. (You heard me right.) It not only attracts other guests away from the party but also is just plain rude. It sends the message to the host that the guest would rather be home watching TV! And it makes the host wish he were.

The next time this happens, march right over to the TV as if it were a household pest you needed to get rid of. Say something like, "I wonder how this thing got turned on." Then turn it off and hide the remote control under your pillow in the bedroom. As an added precaution, whenever possible stand in front of the TV during your mingling, so as to block it from view.

If any one of your guests repeats this behavior after doing it once and seeing your reaction, never invite him to your house again.

(Note: There are two exceptions to this hard and fast rule. The first is if someone telephones to tell you that you or one of your guests is unexpectedly appearing on TV for some reason, and the second is if there is a national emergency—and I mean like a nuclear bombing, not the O. J. verdict.)

The Problem of Relativity: Family Horrors

Some people believe that before we are born into this world we actually get to choose who our families will be, so that we will have just the right combination of partners and teachers around us for our spiritual growth during this particular lifetime. It's a compelling theory, but I don't see how it can be true when we look at how much our relatives embarrass us in social situations.

Take the time my friend's great aunt Alice interrupted a dinner party by wandering into the dining room and asking where her Depends were; the time another friend's tipsy father went up to his new son-in-law just as they were cutting the wedding cake to demand just what the heck his damned intention was toward his daughter anyway; or the memorable occasion on which my five-year-old nephew asked an elderly lady I was interviewing when she was going to die, because he could tell from all the wrinkles in her face that she was *so* old. If one of your friends behaved like this you could conveniently forget to send out his or her invitation next time around. But family members are like tatoos; they may embarrass you, but you are more or less stuck with them.

Dear Miss Mingle:

At parties, I've noticed my father, a retired pilot, asking people with a kind of grim purpose whether or not they know how to fly airplanes. Usually they say no and become flustered as he proceeds to give them a detailed explanation of what flying a plane—say, a Cessna 182— involves. Can you suggest ways in which mingling incidents such as these may be smoothed over?

Mortified in Missouri

Dear Mortified:

If it makes you feel any better, I know someone whose grandmother believes her stuffed dog is a live dog and feeds it mashed potatoes and other messy foods at dinner. My best advice to you is to do what this grandmother's family does: Ignore it as much as possible. You can't control your father's behavior—only your own.

However, if you should happen to be standing right there with your father when this happens, you can always gently interrupt his litany with something like, "My father is just crazy about planes, as you can see." Make a quick segue: "Now me—I'm just plain crazy!" or "Now me—I'm crazy about this smoked salmon. Have you tried it?" Then try to take charge of the conversation by asking your father's victim lots of questions about something you know will interest him.

On the other hand, you could just go make yourself a double martini and not worry about it.

Dear Miss Mingle:

When I am home with my family, there are always tons of people around. My mother gives lots of parties, some of them extended family affairs and some for friends and family. I'm forced to mingle for days on end. How can I avoid the constant socializing without offending anyone?

O.D.'ed on Mingling

Dear O.D.'ed:

You have a much rarer disease than minglephobia: *mingletosis*, which is caused by too much mingling. While you are with your family, take one or more of the following cures:

• Pretend to be sick (which won't be a lie, since you are suffering from severe mingletosis) and stay in bed with a book for a day or two.

• Offer to go out to the store(s) for supplies everyday. Take a long time shopping.

• Go to the beauty parlor or a local health spa; have your hair done; have your nails done; get a pedicure or a massage. (Apologize sweetly for missing whatever family event you miss but explain you just *really* needed it.)

• Arrange in advance to have some "business meetings" or "personal friend crises" that will call you away from the house often. Again, apologize profusely to your relatives and pretend that while you would much rather be having cocktails (again!) with them, it just couldn't be helped.

• Meditate every morning before you come down to breakfast. This will help keep you centered and energetic.

• Take up smoking. Smoking is such a leprous thing to do nowadays that you will be constantly forced to go off by yourself to indulge.

Dear Miss Mingle:

My wife and I regularly host dinner parties that are marked by witty and literate conversations from all in attendance except when HE attends. HE is my bride's father, whose lack of awareness that he is boring the hell out of everyone else is made worse by the fact that he is hard of hearing and won't get a hearing aid. We would tell him to shut up, but that would probably not work because he would not take us seriously. How should we handle this, both with "Dad," and with our friends?

One important note: There is no significant inheritance at risk.

Harried and Hungry

Dear Harried and Hungry:

Conventional wisdom will tell you that you and your spouse should on these occasions work very hard to make sure your father-in-law doesn't dominate the company. For example, ask your guests many questions about themselves and interrupt your father-in-law as much as possible with things like, "Please pass the peas." But if I were you, I would simply not invite my friends when HE is coming to dinner. When you have invited HIM, invite other family members only, or invite people who are extremely tolerant, deaf, or both. Or seat HIM next to your most good natured (or least favorite!) guest, and thank the guest afterward for putting up with HIM.

A good thing to keep in mind is that often people's relatives are annoying to them when no one else even notices that there is a problem. Perhaps you are being overly sensitive as to the effect of this relative.

On the other hand, there's always the old folks home.

On Shaky Ground: Delicate Situations

In the realm of social interaction, having difficult relatives is sometimes the least of your worries. Some mingling situations are virtual mine fields by their very nature and call for a light touch; and sometimes unexpected things happen, and you suddenly find yourself in what is—at least to you—unchartered territory.

One night I gave a dinner party for six. When one of the couples arrived (let's call them Joe and Jane) it was obvious something was very wrong between them. When they went in the other room to put down their coats, I pulled my friend Judy aside and asked her what was up.

"They've just split," she whispered. "They're only here together because they didn't want to ruin your dinner party."

Now I don't mind telling you that after hearing this I felt that my dinner party was really on shaky ground. However, blessedly, we all managed to get through the evening without any major catastrophes, even though the atmosphere was a little tense at times. I tried not to ask Joe or Jane any direct questions, and successfully steered the conversation away from relationship-oriented topics.

Judy stayed to help me clean up. I was congratulating myself on how well it had all gone (considering) when I noticed Judy had a funny look on her face.

"Why are you looking like that?" I demanded. "Don't you think everyone enjoyed their dinner?"

"Oh, sure," Judy said, "What they had of it."

"What do you mean?"

Judy laughed. "Darling, you never served anything but the first course." She was right, I realized in horror. I had been so nervous about getting through the evening I had forgotten the main course, the salad, and the dessert and had rushed all my guests out the door at 9:00!

I had leftovers for days.

Dear Miss Mingle:

I met this attractive woman at a party last week, and we really seemed to hit it off. I don't usually do well meeting people at parties, so I was really excited.

Anyway, we'd been talking for about fifteen minutes, and I was just about to ask for her phone number when I noticed she had some food stuck between her teeth. It was a big piece of green gunk, probably spinach. I gestured with my finger and told her she had something caught there.

Well, she covered her mouth with her hand and sprinted away from me as if I'd just said she was on fire or something. I stayed at the party for a while longer, thinking she'd get over it, and I could resume talking to her, but she continuously avoided me. I don't get it. I mean, I'd want to know if I had food stuck between my teeth.

What did I do wrong?

Baffled in Buffalo

Dear Baffled:

Well for heaven's sake! There is nothing like a little humiliation to throw cold water on a warm conversation. Just because you would want to know doesn't mean everyone would.

I realize it can be quite horrible to have to endure the sight of strange green matter in someone else's mouth, but you have got to decide if it isn't better, when all is said and done, than looking at no mouth at all. And even though, in all likelihood, the woman is bound to discover this dental disfigurement herself later—and wonder, horrified, how many people had seen it—this is still preferable to actually being confronted with her condition, especially just when she thought she was appearing so attractive to you.

In general, only a good friend should feel free to

point out such an extremely yucky faux pas. What you *should* have done was to have ignored it completely, or to have gotten the unfortunate woman a drink in the hopes of an accidental tooth wash.

Try never to forget that—in mingling, at least— honesty is a highly overrated policy.

Dear Miss Mingle:

Help quick!! My boss is having a little luncheon (it's starting in fifteen minutes, so hurry!) where we are all going to meet his new boyfriend (my boss is gay). I'm a straight single woman, and although I have no problem with my boss being gay, I have a little problem with the fact that his new boyfriend is my old boyfriend. My boss doesn't know this. What kind of small talk can I make? How do I keep my fettucini down?

Baked in the Big Apple

Dear Baked in the Big Apple:

Ah, modern life. Ain't it grand? Here are some DO's and DON'Ts which might help someone else in your shoes, since this reply obviously comes too late for you:

DON'T bring up things that tip off anyone at lunch that you and the boss's new flame were ever anything to each other. Comments like "Remember that boat trip we took last summer?" are most definitely out.

DON'T sit next to him, if you can avoid it. Sit as far away as possible.

DON'T try to wash down your fettucini with alcohol. You never know what will come back up ("Hey Boss, ask Ronnie to show you the funny mole on his left hip.").

DO talk as little as possible.

DO go immediately from lunch to your therapist.

Dear Miss Mingle:

I don't know who to turn to for help with my problem. I'm embarrassed to talk to friends about it, but it seems too trivial a matter to seek professional help. Whenever I am introduced to a man at a party, for some reason I can't stop myself from staring at his hair to see if he is wearing a toupee or has a hair weave or some other hair enhancement product. Several men have noticed my doing this, I'm sure of it, but have been too polite to ask why my eyes keep darting up to the top of their heads. What can I do? Please help me rid my mind of this mingling distraction.

Wigged Out in Wisconsin

Dear Wigged Out:

Actually, dear, I think you *may* in fact need professional help. But until you get it:

How about saying, "I know I keep looking at your hair, but I can't help it; I used to be a hair stylist." Or: "Mmmm...Are you wearing a toupee? I know it's unusual, but I have this *thing* about balding men. I'm ashamed to say I can't keep my hands off them."

Dear Miss Mingle:

This may be a rather indelicate question, but how do you handle a coworker who insists on discussing business through the bathroom stall door when you are trying to answer nature's call—in privacy?

Stalling for Time

Dear Stalling for Time:

It's always hard to end a conversation—or escape—when you are physically unable to walk away. However, the situation you describe is one of the most awkward. You'd think people would have a better sense of personal boundaries, but today's world is so fast-paced that people conduct business anywhere, anytime. I know someone who even heard a man talking on his cordless (phone) while on the john.

Perhaps you can use one the following Bathroom Buzz-Off Lines:

"Let's talk about that when I get back to my office."

"Do we have to discuss that this second?"

"Listen, you may not have noticed it, but we are in the men's room."

"Uh, I'm in private conference in here, Jim."

"Look, I've got my own business to take care of at the moment. Do you mind?"

As a last resort, make retching noises. (Or other noises which Miss Mingle won't name.)

Dear Miss Mingle:

What do you do when you arrive at a restaurant where you are supposed to meet a friend, and she has, without telling you, brought someone along who you don't like? This happened to me recently, and I was so taken aback I couldn't even speak for a half hour. We had arranged this dinner date two weeks ahead of time, and I had a lot of personal matters I wanted to discuss with my friend. I told her afterward that I was angry about it, and she acted surprised. She said she thought that we would all have a lovely time together and so she just arranged it.

My question has two parts: First, do you think what she did was okay? And second, once I was at the restaurant, what were my options? Could I have made some excuse to leave? How does one get through such an evening?

Double-Booked and Double-Crossed

Dear Double-Booked:

I absolutely abhor this kind of thing. Whether the perpetrator of this faux pas has double-booked by mistake and figures a "group date" is the best way to deal with it, or whether she is innocently and altruistically trying to put two of her friends together; it is still thoughtless and inconsiderate. You are left to wonder if your popular friend really ever wanted to have dinner with you at all—maybe she invited the other person so she wouldn't be bored. Or, you may think, perhaps she got a second invitation—after yours—from a person she preferred to see, but she couldn't quite get up the nerve to cancel you at the last minute.

Unfortunately, whatever the reason for this woman's bad manners, you must try endure the evening cheerfully—or at least politely—lest you make a bad situation worse. Try to stash away your annoyance until later on, and make some effort to enjoy whatever this third person has to offer. If, as you say, you really dislike this other person, it is perfectly acceptable to beg off early, pleading a headache or an early meeting.

To save yourself from this unpleasant experience in the future, always check with this person, (if indeed you are sure you want to keep her in your little black book), to make sure you know the plan. If she's done it once, she's likely to do it again. Before any rendezvous with her, say something like "I am so looking forward to a good, one-to-one chat with you." Or "Will anyone else be there?" If she does want to arrange a threesome or a group thing in advance, that is perfectly fine, of course, as long as she tells you beforehand. She might even have some friends or acquaintances you *would* enjoy meeting.

Dear Miss Mingle:

What do you do when you run into someone at a party who fired you and ruined your life? This happened to me, and I wanted to deck the guy, but I had a drink in one

*hand and a cracker in the other so I couldn't. I ended up
not speaking to him at all, which was not just awkward
but was also definitely not satisfying.*

All Fired Up

Dear All Fired Up:

Amy Vanderbilt would no doubt tell you to be polite
or to quietly leave the party if you felt you couldn't be
sociable. But Miss Mingle believes that etiquette should
sometimes take a backseat to emotional survival or
mingling health. Therefore, below are some semiac-
ceptable zingers for your nemesis (which are *under no
circumstances* to be accompanied by any physical act,
except shaking hands).

WARNING: These lines should be delivered either
jovially or with gentle irony and definitely without a
tone of bitterness. Try to keep calm at all times.

"Hello there, hatchet man!"

"I'm afraid I can't let you shake my hand; I don't want
to get blood on it."

"Well, well, small world. I hope you're not going to
try to get me thrown out of *here*. I haven't had any hors
d'oeuvres yet."

"Hey, honey, [introducing your wife or husband]
here's the guy who's responsible for my making all
those nice new friends down at the unemployment
office."

(A final note: Keep in mind that getting fired is often a blessing in disguise, and that in corporate America, often the man who does the firing is next on the chopping block.)

Dear Miss Mingle:

I want to know what I should do when someone drags me over to talk to someone who I know doesn't want to talk to me—either because they are already involved in conversation or because I know they don't like me. I have a friend who does this to me all the time. I know he is only trying to get me to talk to people, but it embarrasses me and I never know how to handle it.

Pushed Around in P-town

Dear Pushed Around:

One should never feel embarrassed for something that is not in one's control (in a perfect world, one would never feel embarrassed, period). I am sure it is obvious to the interrupted parties that the interruption was not your doing. Be polite, say hello, chat for a few minutes, and then excuse yourself as quickly as you want. Because you did not approach them of your own accord, you have no obligation to remain for more than a minute or two.

As for people not liking you, are you sure about this? Minglephobia and paranoia are often closely linked. Also, sometimes we imagine people don't like us and we are misreading them altogether. I only recently found out that someone I knew in college used to think I was a total snob, when what was really happening was that I needed glasses and couldn't see people's faces. When this person walked by me, I wouldn't say hello because I didn't recognize her!

P.S. I am sure your strong-arming friend means well and that he is just trying to grease the mingling wheels. But if you know him well enough, take him aside sometime (not at a party) and tell him you appreciate his trying to help, but that you'd rather he didn't treat you like a shuttlecock.

Business or Pleasure?

I must admit that my ideas about socializing at the office were somewhat skewed by repeated childhood viewings of the movie *Desk Set*, with Katharine Hepburn and Spencer Tracy. The 1957 movie features a drunken Christmas party, complete with bongo drums, wild dancing, and lots of other unofficelike behavior like smooching with mail-room guys right out in the open—while kindly bosses look on.

Imagine my intense disappointment to discover upon reaching adulthood that one is never supposed to let loose like this at the office, and that for the most part, office parties are either dull or nerve-wracking affairs. Socializing at the office must always be done very carefully, since good relationships with coworkers are essential to your very existence.

I guess it's not hard to figure out why I no longer work in an office.

Dear Miss Mingle:

Every few weeks or so our office gets together for drinks. Last time, a coworker who I find very attractive was eating a piece of shrimp as she was talking to me, and it dropped down her décolletage. My first instinct was to try to follow it, an instinct that I of course did not act on. How can I tell if she was just being sloppy or was sending me a message, and if she was sending me a message, what was it?

Wondering in Wichita

Dear Wondering:

The answer could be both. That she was being sloppy, but that subconsciously she was sending you a message. However, you cannot assume anything in a situation like this. I spill things on my blouse all the time and I don't *think* it's because I want people to grab me.

Usually it's not that hard to tell the difference between clumsiness and seduction, if happy hour hasn't dulled your radar too much. However, if it were to happen again and you think your coworker won't be offended, try a test question such as:

"Do you need help retrieving that?" or (a little more wicked) "Do you think some day I might be able to switch places with that piece of shrimp?" Her response to one of these should tell you a lot. (If she slaps your face or walks away, the mystery is solved.)

WARNING: Whether she is interested in you or not, be very careful about flirting with or dating people from the office. It can get even messier than spilled shrimp.

Dear Miss Mingle:

My husband and I recently got together with another couple for dinner. The other woman works for the same company as my husband (and, in fact, was his supervisor at one time). As usual, the conversation remained primarily business related and primarily between my husband and this woman. What clever thing can I say in this situation to steer the conversation away from business and on to more interesting things?

Left Out in Los Angeles

Dear Left Out:

It *is* a bit rude for two people at a table of four to talk about anything that by its nature excludes the other two—and that includes "shop talk." If trying to change the subject in the usual fashion doesn't work ("Doesn't that lamb look delicious," "So how are the kids?"), try to think of a subject that would interest everyone—a new local ordinance, a local news event, or an ethical dilemma. (These are always good when you're desperate: "Listen, can I ask all of you what you would do in this situation? I am so confused about it....")

When all else fails, drop one of the following gentle hints:

"Hey guys, didn't you see the sign on the door as we came in? NO SHOP TALK."

"What are you two trying to do, make this dinner a tax write-off?"

"If you all don't stop talking business, Jim and I may run off and have an affair."

Dear Miss Mingle:

During a business lunch with a very friendly and open colleague, is it appropriate to broach personal topics, or should one stick to more general matters in order to maintain the professional relationship unsullied by "true confessions"?

Looking for the Lunch Line

Dear Looking for the Lunch Line:

The answer to this question depends a lot on just what your business relationship is. If you are dining with your boss you should try to avoid talking about your personal life unless he or she asks about it. On the other hand, if you and your colleague are on equal footing, by all means get personal—it's usually more relaxing and therefore goes better with food. To discuss only business would make lunch pretty hard to swallow. Do be sure, however, not to talk about your fiancé's sexual prowess or your mother's problem with heroin unless you feel you are *really* close friends. There is still a delicate balance to be struck with pals from the office, and you never know when your lunchtime confidences will become grapevine fodder.

Kid Stuff

The third most popular topic of conversation in America is kids.* (The first is sex, and the second is money—except of course in New York City, where the first is real estate.) People just love to talk about their children, and they will usually never tire of the subject. Even if you don't have children, you can win over any parents, anywhere, any time by saying nice things about *their* children. And, in fact, it's not hard to say nice things about children because children are wonderful. They are in the state of being "human" we all secretly want to be in: innocent, inquisitive, honest, imaginative, unique, and nonjudgmental.

On the other hand, combine a lot of adults and a lot of children together in one place and you can get: noise, confusion, competition, breakage, and violence. (And, sure, sometimes a lot of fun, too.)

*(Don't anyone quote me; I just made that up.)

Dear Miss Mingle:

My little girl (she's two and a half) and I were at an afternoon open house at a friend-neighbor's when a boy about her age came over and grabbed her graham cracker away from her. I asked him to give it back, but he wouldn't, and when I asked his father to ask him, he wouldn't. He said something to the effect of "Oh, they're okay." In the meantime, my daughter kept crying, and the little boy took a bite, ran into the living room, and then dropped the rest of it on the floor.

It's not the cracker as much as the principle of the thing. How does one remain civil with a father like that? Is there something I can say to him or should I just snub him?

Piqued Papa

Dear Piqued Papa:

In a party situation like this, I'm afraid it is a mistake to make an issue of this type of incident, however disturbing. All you can do is to try to protect your child as much as possible from further attacks. It may make you feel better to find a sympathetic fellow parent at the party who either saw the cracker caper or who will listen to your story. There will be some satisfaction gained in both of you thoroughly 'dissing' the feckless father and agreeing that he should have his parent license revoked.

Dear Miss Mingle:

What can you do when your child repeats something he has overheard you say about another person in front of that person? My seven-year-old son has a great memory. He always seems to innocently come out with something awful I have told my husband about somebody we know. This can be really mortifying. Last week we had a neighbor over for dinner, and my son asked her, "Are you the lady who never takes a bath?"

Of course, we shouldn't be gossiping, I realize that, but we're only human. Any suggestions?

Ashamed in Asheville

Dear Ashamed:

I myself have been the object of several such excruciating "juvenilely transmitted" faux pas. In some cases the parent can cover up by correcting the child and by pretending the child has just somehow got it all wrong. But this is not an altogether honest face to show the child. I hate to say it, but the best thing you can do is to try to wait until your child goes to bed before dishing the dirt.

Dear Miss Mingle:

I am the father of a beautiful six-month-old daughter. When I take her to parties with me, which I do on occasion, we often have a throng of people around us because she is so cute.

The problem is, while this may sound strange coming from a proud papa, I am actually getting tired of talking only about how much my daughter looks like her mother, how small her fingers are, and why she might be smiling at any given moment. I happen to have a very interesting career as well as many interesting leisure pastimes (scuba diving, photography, and skiing, to name a few).

How can I change the subject without seeming like a rotten, non-nineties dad? (Am I a rotten, non-nineties dad?)

Bored With Baby-Talk

Dear Bored With Baby-Talk:

I don't know whether you are a rotten dad or not, but since Miss Mingle is not here to judge you but to help you, you can do one of three things:

1. If your baby's mother is not in the picture or doesn't feel like holding your daughter, hand her off to one of the admiring females—many women like to hold the baby, any baby—and go and mingle unencumbered. Without the cutey-pie in your arms, the subject won't be so all consuming, although it *will* still come up in conversation.

2. Become adept at changing subjects. For example, when person X remarks how much your little bundle of joy looks like her mother, ask X who X looked like when *she* was a baby, then lead the conversation around to old

photographs (in which your person X resembled either her own father or mother), and then move on to one of your favorite topics, photography. You might have to work at honing your subject-changing skill, but it sounds as though it may be worth it for you.

3. As usual, Miss Mingle's favorite option comes in the form of a fib. After the second or third remark, question, or compliment about your daughter, say, "You know I love hearing this, and you *know* there is nothing I would rather do than talk about her all night long, but I just read this article in a parenting journal that claims that even at six months it's not healthy for her to always be the center of attention and to be hearing constant compliments." (Smile down at your daughter) "But we do appreciate it, don't we, precious?" (Now shift your daughter's position on your body slightly, and look back up at your conversational partner) "So. Tell me what's new with you at the agency. . . . "

Dear Miss Mingle:

I don't know whether I am living in the dark ages or what, but I often find myself in the awkward position of trying to let people know that when I invite them to my house I am not inviting their kids. People nowadays seem to think it quite natural to bring along their eighteen month old and four year old to your cocktail party. Sure, baby-sitters are expensive, and a lot of working parents can't bear further separation from their children, but isn't it inconsiderate to inflict your children on other people's parties?

You may not believe it when I say I really love kids (I really do), but I think there is a place for adult-only fun, too. How can I make it clear to people without offending them that my invitation isn't for the little ones?

                                        Puzzled Party-Giver

Dear Puzzled Party-Giver:

While I feel for some parents, I have to say that I agree with you that unless it is otherwise specified, kids are usually not invited. One should always take care to note what is written on an invitation. In other words, if the invitation is addressed to "The Williams Family," then the kids *are* invited, and if it says "Mr. and Mrs. Williams," the kids *are not* invited. In general, children are included in afternoon gatherings starting before 5:00 P.M.

However, while in most suburbs (where there are more inexpensive baby-sitters and more stay-at-home moms) this rule is still generally understood, it is quite a different story in major metropolitan areas. And because you can no longer be sure that people will follow the old rule, if you don't want children at any party (even a dinner party) you must find a way to stipulate that fact during the invitation process. Never assume that just because you have told the parents you are having a bathtub-gin-rock-and-roll party complete with nude dancers that they will show up without their children.

I know of several methods, some subtle, some not, to

make sure your guests "get it." One ploy is to tell people your house is not childproof. Another is to say, "By popular demand from most of the parents I know, this party is going to be for adult relaxation and everyone is leaving their kids at home."

Yet another, more dishonest method is to make up a "bad child" story. "There's one particular child of someone who is invited—I don't want to say who—anyway this child is so bad I just can't have him in my house. I had to make a No Children rule so the mother wouldn't bring him."

I know there are a lot of parents out there who are reading this and saying, "What is she talking about? I would never bring my kids to an adult party. What fun would that be?" And to those parents, I say: Oops. Never mind. (And hope that I haven't given you any ideas.)

****

A Quick Quiz for Parents:

Sometimes it is difficult to tell whether or not your children are included in an invitation to a particular social function, especially if the invitation is given in person or by phone. When you are unsure, which of the following should you say to your host-to-be?:

A. "Should I bring little Stevie?"

B. "I'm afraid I may not be able to bring my kids."

C. "We'd love to come. I'll have to see if I can line up a baby-sitter."

Answer: C is the best answer. It allows your host to say, "Oh please, bring Stevie along—it's a family affair." Or "Good, I hope you can [get a baby-sitter]." The next best answer is B, because if kids are *not* invited at least the host can respond, "Well, that *is* too bad, but it may be just as well as it wouldn't have been very much fun for him." To the last choice A the host is forced to reply "No, don't bring him; kids aren't invited," which will make the him feel like an ogre.

****

Dear Miss Mingle:

As a relatively new mother, I was stymied recently when I came to collect my two year old from nursery school. In one fell swoop, I was greeted by my son with a huge, bleeding bite mark on his cheek; his distraught teacher saying, "You might want to take him to the doctor....Susie did it"; and Susie herself—wearing a sly, satisfied smile.

Before I could gather my wits, in strode Susie's attorney mother. Somehow, when the dust had settled, I realized that I'd inanely muttered, "Gee, it's okay." But it wasn't!

Short of litigation, how might I have more satisfactorily registered my shock-horror-dismay without having turned the nursery school into an even more gory battlefield?

Meek Mommy

Dear Meek Mommy:

It's always very difficult—almost impossible—to know how to act when you are in this position. On one hand, your child has been brutally attacked; and on the other hand these things do happen. And even though the mishap is possibly the result of faulty upbringing, the mother did not (I assume) sic her kid on yours intentionally. The perfect tone to use with this mother, if you can find the emotional equilibrium to project it, lies somewhere within the wide gap between polite and outraged. Instead of mumbling to the attorney mom, "It's okay," how about one of the following:

"Don't worry, I'll let you know how he is doing after I

take him to the emergency room. I'm sure you and little Susie will want to know."

"I'm sure he'll be fine. It's just that he's never been bitten before."

"I'm sure it'll heal—eventually."

"I don't think any permanent damage was done. But if you don't mind a little friendly advice, Dr. Spock has an *excellent* chapter on children who bite. You and your husband might want to take a look at it."

"Listen, if we decide to sue, at least you won't have to hire a lawyer."

Dear Miss Mingle:

I think I am pretty typical as a mother. What I mean is that I am very proud of my two children, and I admit I love to talk about them. (They are both exceptionally smart and good-looking.) My problem is this: Sometimes I think other mothers talk about their children too much, describing every little thing they do and every little thing they say. How do I make certain I'm not doing the same thing? The last thing I want to be is another bragging parent.

Pom Pom Mom

Dear Pom Pom Mom:

Forget about it. The words *bragging* and *parent* are synonymous. Being convinced your child hung the moon is an emotional condition of motherhood you can't escape. Nature set it up to be this way, so don't fight it.

Dear Miss Mingle:

Last month I was invited to a baby shower held for my goddaughter, whose baby is due in six weeks. It would have been quite a lovely afternoon if it weren't for several young mothers present, who, without any preamble, proceeded to unbutton their blouses and breast-feed their babies in plain sight of everyone in the room.

It's true I was raised in more conservative times, but I find it appalling that women today do not breast-feed their infants in private. I feel that if they were to excuse themselves and retire to a quiet room, it would not only be a healthier experience for the baby but for the poor, unsuspecting guests as well.

Horrified Great-Godmother

Dear Horrified:

This is one of those areas of etiquette where what is acceptable to one generation may not be at all acceptable to another. If a group of women are all comfortable about breast-feeding "en masse," then it certainly seems okay to me for them to do so. (Maybe I should have written a chapter called Mingling While Milking.) However—and this is a very strong however—if there are others present who feel it is inappropriate behavior, as you do, the nursing moms should respect that and remove themselves from the general party area. Breast-feeding is a very intimate matter and breast-feeders should make an effort to be aware of how it affects bystanders.

Most important, grandparents and godparents are always to be given the highest amount of respect possible, from my point of view.

Menagerie à Trois:
Pet Peeves

I was on the phone with my friend Ted one day and was telling him about a nerve-wracking luncheon I had gone to, during which the host's Irish setter had not stopped nuzzling me the whole time. The dog kept coming up from behind and sticking his head under my armpit. "Not only was it pretty irritating, but it made it extremely hard to eat my vichyssoise." I told Ted.

"Hmm...interesting." Ted said, a superior kind of knowing tone in his voice.

"What do you mean, 'Interesting'?" I asked, rather annoyed.

"Don't you know," he replied smugly, "that whatever an animal does to you is what its owner wants to do to you?"

"Oh come *on,*" I protested, remembering with mounting horror all the humping, peeing, biting, and licking I had endured from various pets I had known.

"It's a widely accepted fact," Ted insisted.

"Are you trying to tell me the host wanted to smell my armpit?" I said.

"Something like that," Ted said. "But don't feel bad. Last week my cat clawed my mother right in the crotch."

"Uh-oh."

"Uh-oh is right. It sent me right back to my shrink."

"What did your shrink say?"

"She said I should get the cat declawed."

"There! What did I tell you," I yelled into the phone triumphantly, "Your theory is all nonsense!"

"No it's not," Ted said calmly. "My shrink's in denial about this. She's very hostile toward me."

"Why do you say that?" I asked him.

"Her parakeet keeps glaring at me."

Dear Miss Mingle:

At our country estate, our cat has a nasty habit of bringing mice and chipmunks in from the outside to give to me (because he loves me). This would be disgusting enough if the critters weren't often still alive and didn't try to dash off behind the furniture when the cat puts them down. My wife sometimes has employed a skillet and a shoe to bean the poor mice, leaving me the task of picking up their dead little bodies and throwing them in the forsythia. But just the other evening, the cat brought a live field mouse into the dining room where eight people were about to sit down to an elegant dinner and I wasn't sure how to respond.

Since some people tend to look askance at mice in the house, and since our antique furniture may not be solid enough to hold the people who want to jump up on it to escape, what is a host to do? After all, the cat lives here too, and has some rights, but the guests are guests.

P.S. Talking to the cat has not seemed to work.

Facing CATastrophe

Dear Facing CATastrophe:

My cat Scarlett used to like to hide half-eaten birds inside shoes (sometimes guests' shoes), so I know how you feel. The proper thing to do is to warn the guests—in as nondescriptive a way as possible—what may be in store for them feline-wise. In addition to this, make efforts to keep the cat out of the dining room, so that at least the guests won't be treated to the disconcerting sight of the cat with something wriggling in its mouth while they are actually eating, which, to my way of thinking, would be the worst possible scenario.

Your only alternative to this is to put a bell on the cat, but as a fellow cat lover, I can't recommend this. But by all means, keep talking to your cat; maybe one day you'll get through to it.

Dear Miss Mingle:

Recently my closest girlfriend married a wonderful man who has a pet male chimpanzee named Clamp, which is what he does to me whenever I visit. It's not just sexual (which is bad enough), he also continually brings me offerings like fruit, lightbulbs, and Minute rice. Whenever I go to their apartment—which is often but growing less frequent—Clamp is all over me. Yesterday he attacked me from behind and stuffed a grape up my nose.

My friend says it's just "his way," but I think it's more serious than his just being playful, especially since I can see he is not that way with anyone else. What can I do about this pushy primate? Clamp is becoming more and more amorous and insistent, and I fear I will have to stop seeing my friend, who finds it all rather amusing. (She actually asked me if Clamp had asked me out for New Year's Eve!)

Going Ape

Dear Going Ape:

Your letter really raised my fur. Besides having no patience with people who can't control their pets, I really hate to see a fellow single woman being fobbed off on an animal. As soon as you can, go to your neighborhood pet store and inquire about chimpanzee repellent. If they can't help you, go to the library and read up on what turns the horrid things off. If it's some smelly disgusting thing that will leave an odor in the house of this supposed friend of yours, so much the better. In fact, if there is no known antidote to chimp lust, try this: Next time you go there for a meal, and Clamp begins his ritual offerings to you, grab whatever he has given you, scream as loudly as you can, and throw it on the floor. Then jump up and down on it, stamping furiously. If the stubborn beast still persists, push him off you onto the floor, still screaming as loudly as you can. I think that's how a female chimp says no (I saw it in a movie once). Keep throwing whatever he gives you to the floor, even if it's the couple's best bone china.

Don't worry about your friend and her husband, who will be watching all this paralysed and open mouthed. Anyone with an over-amorous pet monkey deserves a little Tarzan performance with their soup.

Dear Miss Mingle:

The other day someone told me that the pet food section of the grocery store is a great place to mingle. If this is true, how is it done? Do you just park your cart there and lean against the shelves, or what?

Coupon Don Juan

Dear Coupon Don Juan:

Actually, while *mingling* might not be the most accurate description for it, the pet food section is not a bad place to meet people. Fate has to help out a little, because you definitely should not "lean against the shelves" and hang out. If no one comes along within ten or fifteen minutes (at the most), you need to move on. But you can, if you want, spend a fairly long time looking at different kinds of cat and dog food, comparing prices, and reading ingredient labels, until someone else who looks interesting comes along to select *her* pet food. Then you simply make a remark about a certain type of food, or ask her advice on what food to buy. Ask what kind of pet she has, how old it is, etc. If you have a pet, you know how much people like to talk about their pets. We're much worse than parents with their children.

I have actually met some very interesting people in the pet food section. I once even dated a guy I met in the pet food section of a grocery store in Chicago. Unfortunately, like his pet, he turned out to be nothing but a hound dog.

Travelogues: Tips for Trips

One of the things that makes traveling exciting is that you never know who you are going to meet on a trip. Once, on my way to Paris, I met a rather cocky photo-journalist (at least he said he was one; people tend to make up things about themselves while traveling because it is so easy to get away with) who informed me that he had a glass eye. He told me he had lost his real eye covering some Third World skirmish—and then what did he proceed to do but pop it out right then and there to prove it to me! I believe this was one of the only times I have been at a loss for words. I just yelped and covered my face. (Although later, as we were getting off the plane, I did manage to quip, "Be sure to keep one eye on the luggage.")

Traveling affords many wonderful opportunities for meeting people. It is, in fact, one of the few times when it is always absolutely acceptable to talk to strangers, because that's all there are. When you add to this implicit license for conversational promiscuity the romance of people going to different places for unknown reasons, you have a fertile mingling ground indeed. So why is it that so many people fail to take advantage of it?

Dear Miss Mingle:

I was on a train one Friday afternoon comfortably ensconced in my travel style, which includes a double seat all to myself, lots of reading material, and food to nibble on. I welcome these trips because they offer an opportunity for naps or a sustained period of silent contemplation. Unfortunately this outlook tends to restrict social interactions to the ticket punch of the conductor. Even though I am a frequent user of mass transit, I can count on one hand the number of conversations I have had with other passengers.

On this particular train, I noticed a woman sitting across the aisle from me. Like me, she was carrying the sort of travel bag that indicated a weekend trip. Over the course of the ride, we exchanged glances, but to interpret these as anything other than coincidental seemed farfetched. Knowing how much I usually enjoy my own privacy, it seemed inappropriate to invade hers. And even if she had seemed approachable, my own internal brakes kept me from making any overture: What would I say that would seem intelligent, interesting, not just another come-on? Once I started the conversation, how would I con-clude it? Would I get bored several minutes into it? Did I really care about the book she was reading? Was talking to someone I would probably never see again worth the effort?

As the train pulled into the station, we collected our possessions. She moved ahead and departed in a crowd. Our chance for dialogue was lost.

You will no doubt infer from my tale that I am some-what introverted and shy. The obvious conversation breakers (How is that book? Are you visiting for the weekend? Long train ride, huh?) are too stiff for me. Please advise this hopeless minglephobe.

Untrained and Derailed

Dear Untrained and Derailed:

Unfortunately, many people avoid conversing with their fellow passengers because: like you, they are busy and stressed and use travel time for quiet time; and as you also suggest, it can seem dangerous to strike up a conversation from which it may be hard to escape.

First of all, you must decide whether or not you really are open to mingling on the train. It sounds to me as if you purposely arrange yourself to make meeting peo-ple hard, then wistfully stare at whoever is across the aisle. Why not make room for mingling—and make room for your destiny. Once you have made it impossible for anyone to take the seat next to you, your chances of having a conversation with a fellow passenger are pretty slim. If you and your potential conversational partner are both in adjacent aisle seats (and for some reason neither one of you wants to talk to your *own* seatmate) it is possible, but pretty awkward. As for subject matter, travel creates some easy ones:

Destination: Asking a person where she is headed is always an acceptable and friendly opening, but it must be done within the first few minutes of being together with your seatmate. After you have been sitting together for a certain amount of time, it becomes much harder to break the ice. If you don't make your first contact right away, you may have to wait for something to happen—for the plane to take off, for the food to come, for the conductor to take tickets—in order to make your saying something seem natural. The longer the silence between you continues, the harder it will be to interact.

Commiseration: If there are any problems with the train or plane or bus—lateness, bumpiness, noisy passengers, rude conductors, uncomfortable seats, bad food, broken tray-tables, inordinately loud or crazy passengers, accidents, bad weather, the lights going out—you can easily use them to bond with fellow passengers. People usually *want* to talk to their neighbors about these things because everyone is slightly anxious. (Note: I am talking about a little good-natured complaining here, not excessive whining and bitching or unsetting paranoia—not unless the train actually breaks down.)

Observation: Commenting on what a person is reading, as clichéd as it might be, is simple and effective. (You never want to get caught sneaking a peak at someone's *writing* however. That is considered too intrusive.) Or notice something special about the person's suitcase, hat, or coat. You can also make observations about your surroundings—about the decor ("These trains certainly don't look like they do in old movies."), the annoying flickering fluorescent lights, or about what's outside the train ("Can you believe how hard it's raining out there?").

If you do get stuck in the conversation from hell, as I did once when an elderly lady next to me started telling me about her gum disease, travel-talk escapes aren't as hard as you might think. You can always politely explain that it's been swell chatting but you have work to do before you get to your destination (always have materials ready for this excuse). Or you can get up and go to the café car and not come back to your seat until right before arrival time. And while I sometimes disapprove of Walkmans—I think they isolate people from their environment more than they already are. The Walkman is an excellent escape tool (mine really saved my life on one very hairy bus trip with an antiabortion fanatic). Just don't let the fact that you have one with you keep you from experiencing the possible rewards of talking to a stranger while you travel.

A final note: If you know the train is going to be full, *you* do the seatmate selecting rather than taking a chance at getting someone unappealing next to you. Miss Mingle suggests: avoid people with babies, people who have their laptops open before the train has left the station, and people who smell of alcohol or seem to be talking to themselves. Also try to steer clear of anyone with lots of tape on his eyeglasses.

Dear Miss Mingle:

Recently I was vacationing in the south of France with American friends who live in Paris. A friend of theirs from Germany, whom I had never met before, was already at the house with them when I arrived. He was a pleasant fellow, and we exchanged phone numbers and addresses when he left two days later—in the way one does when traveling.

Last week, my Parisian friends told me that I should expect to hear from this man about a trip he is planning. He is coming to the United States on a visit this winter. Apparently he had called them to ask if my apartment was big enough to accommodate a guest!

While I liked this guy, I don't feel I want to invite a near-stranger into my home as a houseguest. Did I do something wrong? How do I get out of this mess?

No Room at the Inn

Dear No Room at the Inn:

It certainly doesn't sound to me as if you did anything wrong. (It would be quite a different matter if you had stayed in the home of this German.) I assume that your Parisian friends made a noncommittal answer to the fellow's inquiry as to the size and availability of your home; if not, the Parisians are largely to blame for your present predicament. In point of fact, if the Parisians were really friends they should have found a way to let the German know that staying in your apartment was probably not an option.

In any case, know that you are under NO obligation to in any way sponsor this visitor. When he calls, be polite. Ask him out for a drink if you like. Offer to give him directions or information about places to stay and sights to see. But if he hints about your putting him up or asks point blank, use one of the following Houseguest Repellant Lines:

"I'm really sorry, but it's my busy season."

"I'm afraid my schedule won't permit it at this time."

"They're doing some work in my apartment, so it's not a good time for me to have a houseguest."

"I'm sorry but I've already got someone else coming to stay."

"I never have houseguests. I turn into a vampire at night."

****

Miss Mingle Travel Tip

When you are traveling by any mode other than cruise ship, be sure to make only minimum eye contact until your conversation with your seatmate is well underway. Trains, planes, and buses are a bit like elevators—people tend to compensate for the reduced personal space. Because you are in a confined area and forced to sit so closely together, the rules about eye contact are different from what they normally are.

After the initial introduction or exchange of words, avoid looking at your seatmate full in the face for at least ten minutes. Instead, turn slightly toward the person while you are talking to him. An occasional quick glance is okay.

****

Dear Miss Mingle:

I have sort of an antimingling question. Whenever I am on a plane (I travel frequently for business) I seem to always get someone sitting next to me who wants to chat with me during the whole flight. I think people who don't travel a lot see a flight as a romantic time when you meet and talk to exciting strangers; whereas, to me, it's a time to recharge my batteries and have a little peace and quiet before the next event in my life.

How can I discourage conversation with my seatmate without offending the person?

Flying Solo

Dear Flying Solo:

Sometimes talking to strangers is the only way to retain one's sanity on a trip—what with breakdowns, accidents, and terrorist threats—so try to be tolerant of people who need to reach out to someone next to them. They could be nervous, and making small talk makes them feel everything is going to be okay. However, I can also understand your perspective. Even if you were the gregarious type, you can still end up sitting next to someone who drives you crazy.

Your escape routes are limited on a plane. The seats are so small you are practically married to the person next to you by the time you get off. Your only easy escape is work. Make sure you have a book or business papers to immerse yourself in should you get a gabby neighbor. (Magazines don't work as well; for some reason people feel that they can more easily interrupt a magazine reader.) For extreme emergencies, feel free to try one of the more unorthodox methods below:

• Say you are not feeling well and you are unable to converse with anyone.
• Go to sleep (or pretend to).

• Speak in a foreign language (make sure it is an obscure one). You only need to utter a few words, then just shake your head and look confused when the person speaks to you.

• Eat a lot of onions or garlic before you get on the plane.

Working Weddings and Finessing Funerals

Weddings and funerals are both intense social occasions where mingling takes place within the confines of a structured set of rituals. Emotions usually run high, and there are tears shed at both occasions. Because of the nature of these events people who attend them feel the need to do and say the right thing even more keenly than usual. Guests at weddings and funerals are not really guests, but part of the ceremony, and there exists within each person the sense that, like an actor who plays a bit part on stage, his or her behavior is integral to the success of the whole affair.

It is no wonder that people get so nervous at the prospect of making small talk at these festive and solemn ceremonies. It may help you to keep in mind that humans have been gathering together for these two reasons for about as long as we have walked the earth, and that therefore you are certainly not the first person ever to have insulted a bridegroom's mother by asking if she were the caterer, or to have started giggling loudly in the middle of the bereaved brother's teary-eyed eulogy.

Dear Miss Mingle:

My wife and I have been invited to the wedding of one of my wife's coworkers. Other than the two or three people from her company, all of the guests will be complete strangers. What am I going to talk about with these people? And as I will not know a soul in the wedding party aside from the groom (whom I have met only twice); when we go through the receiving line, what clever or interesting thing can I say to them?

Reluctant Wedding Guest

Dear R.W.G.:

One of the most important things to know about mingling at any wedding is that the people standing in the receiving line do not want to be standing in the receiving line. They are tired; they are stressed out; their feet hurt; they are thirsty and hungry, and would rather be sitting down somewhere with a large bottle of champagne. Therefore, what you need to do is to see yourself as an angel of mercy rather than a tongue-tied interloper. Your gift to them: brevity.

Just tell them who you are and move on as quickly as possible. The faster you move through the line, the better they will like you. Don't worry too much about being clever, and don't be afraid to use clichés like "Well, they finally tied the knot." (After all, wedding rituals *are* clichés.) Few people ever remember what someone says in a receiving line anyway.

Pick any of the receiving-line remarks provided at the end of these instructions. In order not to be heard repeating the same remark, you may want to alternate between two or three as you move through the line of people. Greet each person with, "Hello, I'm _____," make your receiving-line remark, and then close cleanly with either "Congratulations" or "So nice to meet [see] you," before moving forward to the next person.

Now here's where there might be a small glitch, in the form of the slowpoke receiving-line guest in front of you who has mistakenly decided this is the time and place for a *real* conversation with one or more of the wedding party members. Since you are under NO circumstances EVER allowed to leapfrog around anyone in a receiving line, you must keep making conversation with your person until you see or sense the slowpoke in front of you moving on. Never move on until you can tell the slowpoke is about to. There's nothing worse than being squashed between two other wedding guests because you have said goodbye without checking to see if the way before you is clear. If you *do* find yourself in this sandwiched position, however, I have found that if you start to move up into the slowpoke's personal space and begin listening in to the conversation, the slowpoke will get the message and move on.

To tell the truth, the hardest thing about the whole receiving-line process is probably the smiling. There is an unwritten law that says that everyone involved must continually smile as hard as they can. By the time you are through—depending on the size of the line—you may have to go somewhere private and massage your cheeks.

Sample Receiving-Line Remarks

"What a beautiful bride!" (So what if everyone says it; the family, who has shelled out $800 for the dress, wants to hear it.)

"My wife works with [name of groom]. We're so glad we could be here today."

"That was the loveliest ceremony I've ever seen." (Never be afraid to overuse superlatives at weddings.)

"You must be so proud! They're both such wonderful people."

"They look so happy.... They really make a perfect couple."

"I know a lot of people have been looking forward to this day."

"I know you've already heard this a million times

but... the music, the flowers, the dresses, the church—everything was just SO beautiful!"

"I see where the bride [the groom] gets her [his] looks!"

As for the mingling during rest of the reception, nobody at weddings knows who everybody is anyway, so don't feel left out. In fact, you can always make your anonymity work for you. If you get bored with the typical wedding talk—which usually revolves around the honored couple's relationship, costumes, honeymoon destination, and future prospects—you might spice things up with some harmless but fun untruths. Once at a friend's wedding, for example, I introduced myself very politely to many people as the groom's personal assistant. (The groom was a carpenter, so this announcement caused a few raised eyebrows.)

P.S. Never thank anyone until you are about to leave the reception, even though it's tempting to do so in the receiving line when you don't know what to say and you are shaking hands with all those parent-host types.

Dear Miss Mingle:

I've had the same socializing problem all my life. I never seem to know what to say to the family of the deceased at funerals. Please help, as funerals are a fact of life and I'll have more to go to as I get older.

Wordless in Williamsburg

Dear Wordless:

The nicest thing about mingling at funerals is that it is your last priority. You are there, after all, to honor the dead publicly, to remember and to say goodby in the privacy of your own heart, and to be comforted and be of comfort to other mourners. Funerals and postfuneral receptions are the only social affairs at which many of the normal rules of mingling are dropped. Everyone is usually on their best behavior, and people are at their most loving. In general, conversations will center around saying nice things about the dead person. (If you don't have anything nice to say about the dead person, don't go to the funeral.) Just remember what you liked most about the deceased—or what was most unique—and share those memories with the survivors.

****

Some Funeral DO's and DON'Ts:

• DO make sure you speak to the bereaved at any postfuneral reception. This can be scary, especially if you are afraid you'll say something to make it more difficult for the grieving person to keep her composure. But it must be done, and will be appreciated. It doesn't matter if all you say is, "I'll miss him."

• DON'T ask any of the deceased's family members what they are planning for the future. Funerals are for looking to the past and for experiencing your feelings in the present.

• DON'T engage in any one-upmanship about the deceased. There is sometimes a ghoulish tendency at funerals for people to try to prove that they knew the dead person better than someone else did. I am often appalled when I go to funerals and hear people saying things to each other like, "But my dear, I just saw her last week—we were practically best friends!"

• DO be sure to offer to help at any social gathering after the funeral unless the affair is catered. If you see any of the deceased's family members looking like they need anything, go up to them and help them out, even if you don't know them well (95 percent of the time help will not be needed, but one should offer).

• DON'T conduct business with people at funerals. There is nothing more gauche.

• DO carry plenty of extra Kleenex in your purse or pocket. Have some to spare.

****

Dear Miss Mingle:

I hope you won't think I'm heartless, but every time I go to a funeral I find myself having such a good time talking to people I haven't seen in a long time that I end up laughing—sometimes sort of loudly—and then I feel that people are looking at me as if I had just committed a major sin or something. I usually feel like the dead person wouldn't mind that I am having a good time, but I guess it is rude to the family. Should I try not to laugh? Should I just stay home rather than risk offending the mourners?

Having Fun at Funerals

Dear Having Fun at Funerals:

As you say, the dead person would probably not mind seeing people having a good time at his funeral, as long as no one is saying mean things about him. However, while laughing is certainly not prohibited, it is a good policy to try to keep the volume down. Unless you are at an Irish wake, raucous laughter may clash with the general tone of the affair, and therefore jangle other people's nerves. Try to be sensitive, but don't beat yourself up about an occasional guffaw; you're only human. Everyone deals with their grief in slightly different fashion, and as long as you are not being disrespectful of the dead or of the occasion, it's okay. Often funerals bring old friends together again, which is a very lovely thing indeed.

On the other hand, if there are mourners sobbing all around you and you're still laughing, you may need to see a psychiatrist.

Mingling in Unusual Places

Mingling with people at cocktail parties and dinner parties is one thing, mingling on crowded subway cars or in the beauty parlor is another. Rules for talking to strangers always change, at least slightly, depending on where the encounter takes place. Nevertheless, it is usually worthwhile to interact with strangers wherever they may be; it's broadening, like travel. You never know when a ten-minute conversation will brighten your whole day. After all, we were not put together on this planet to NOT talk to each other. (At least I know *I* wasn't.)

Dear Miss Mingle:

How do you mingle in the ocean? You may think I'm kidding, but I'm not. I spend much of my summer at the beach, and because I love to swim, I spend a lot of the day in the water. Often I see people in the water who I'd like to talk to. What are the rules about talking to strangers in the water? Is it too weird if I just introduce myself?

Maryland Mermaid

Dear Maryland Mermaid:

The ocean is actually a great place to talk to people, although I have never had a conversation with anyone in the water that ever made it up onto land, if you know what I mean. The reason sea talk is so easy is obvious: You are all doing the same thing, together, which gives you something to talk about (how high are the waves, how cold is the water, was that a dolphin or a shark?). In addition to being involved in a common activity, people are almost always much more relaxed at the beach than they are anywhere else. As a result, people are more open; they let their barriers down and literally go with the flow.

There are a few different guidelines for water mingling: For example, introductions hardly ever happen until after you've been talking for a fairly long time. People rarely use last names in the water. (There is a feeling of anonymity about swimming—possibly because of people being in a semiclothed state.) And escapes are easy—you just ride a wave or quietly sink.

Dear Miss Mingle:

I never know what to do when my dentist starts talking to me while I am in the chair. Usually he has his hands in my mouth, so that if I try to answer him, he has to stop what he is doing. I have noticed he does try to avoid asking me questions that require more than a yes or no response, but most of the time I feel that a yes or no won't suffice. It's hard to keep my responses to Frankenstein-like moans and grunts, which is about all I can manage with someone's hands in my mouth.

I really like my dentist and I like to talk to him, but how can I get him to realize I can't talk with my mouth full of fingers?

All Gummed Up

Dear All Gummed Up:

I think dentists need to be reminded—don't ask me why—that they, in fact, do have their fingers in your mouth and therefore you can't answer. I also think there should be a class they have to take in dental school on conversing with patients.

The way to train your dentist is to just start talking while he's got his hands in there, so that he has to remove them or someone's going to get hurt. (WARNING: Don't try this while there's any drilling or cutting going on.) This will slow him down until, sooner or later, he starts to get the message that he has to be more careful what kinds of questions he asks; or better yet, he'll stop talking to you altogether and pay attention to what he's doing.

Dear Miss Mingle:

A few months ago a coworker invited me to a party where I knew I wouldn't know anyone. I was prepared for this mingling challenge. What I wasn't prepared for was that everyone there was hearing impaired—and signing instead of talking—except for me and the hostess.

Now, I knew beforehand that the hostess had a boyfriend who was deaf, and that therefore there would be other deaf people there, but I wasn't prepared for them all to be hearing impaired. Most of the time I stood in the corner and watched the silent room full of people, feeling totally at a loss. What should I have done?

Dumbstruck

Dear Dumbstruck:

Your choices were indeed limited. If I were you, I would have tried to talk to the hostess as much as I could for an hour or so, and then made it an early evening. Certainly a good hostess in this position—being the only person with whom you could communicate—would not leave you in a corner by yourself. During that hour, I would have tried to get her, as well as any accommodating hearing-impaired guest(s) I could find, to teach me some basic signing. Naturally, you could not have learned enough in one sitting to carry on a real conversation, but your asking would 1) show you were making an effort to talk to the other guests and 2) allow you to go home with a little extra knowledge. And go home I would have, posthaste.

The Unbearable Lightness of Being Naked

For years I thought you had to be thin to go "skinny" dipping. As a result I didn't get in much practice at being naked in a group. This is the excuse I like to use, anyway, for why I find it difficult to socialize while naked, though I have talked to a lot of other people who also get lockjaw as soon as they take it all off. Let's face it, since the Garden of Eden we've been wearing these fig leaves and, darn it, without them most of us are totally rattled. When the protective barrier of clothing is gone, we are no longer sure that the rules of communication remain the same. And, in fact, they don't.

Dear Miss Mingle:

On virtually a daily basis (depending on my energy level), I am faced with a social dilemma that I'm sure affects many other exercise-aholics. What is the appropriate mingling technique in the gym locker room when: 1) you have entered to find a lone naked person ("Good to see you!"); 2) you are alone and unclothed in the locker room when a fully clad person comes in ("So, do you think the weights are doing me any good?"); or 3) both of you are naked ("That's okay, I'll weigh myself after you.")?

I find this situation most difficult when there is only one other person in the locker room. Where do I look? What do I say?

Barely Speaking

Dear Barely Speaking:

The two most important rules for mingling in the buff are: 1) never look at the other person anywhere but in the face, even if you are the naked one and the other person is still fully clothed; and 2) never mention body fat, being overweight, cellulite deposits, pimples, or body hair. (And *never* comment on the attractiveness of a person's undergarments. Even if she *is* wearing a bra and panty set you would kill for.)

In general, extremely intimate situations like saunas and locker rooms call for social interaction to be less personal than normal, in order to counteract the unnatural feeling of familiarity caused by the Nakedness

Factor. There is usually less eye contact of any kind, and your personal-space distance increases. The most comfortable topics for garbless gabs are: the weather; the traffic; complaints about the facilities (The locker room is too hot. The sauna is too cold.); questions about the gym equipment (Are the treadmills crowded? Did you see anyone using the Gravitron today?); and matters of courtesy (Are you using this locker? Excuse me, but you dropped your towel.).

For progressive-minded people who may think I'm being a bit too prudish: It's no use saying we should let it all hang out (so to speak). We live in a dressed world, and unless someone is very unusual or is with a good friend, there *will* be a certain amount of awkwardness. I understand this is less true for men than for women. Reportedly, men have an easier time with what to say to each other when they are undressed, a fact that I would venture to guess has to do—at least in part—with the more communal style of men's rest rooms, and with boys having more exposure in general to locker room situations. The ease with which men are impersonal with each other may also be a result of years of practice in communication *without* intimacy ("How about those Dodgers?"). On the other hand, most women have fairly serious (and unjustified) body-image problems, so they are pretty nervous to be naked in front of anyone, much less able to make small talk.

Do remember that there is certainly no law that says one must converse with nude strangers one encounters in the locker room or anywhere else. It is perfectly acceptable under the circumstances to ignore each other or to make do with a noncommittal "Hi." In fact, this is one time when not talking may be your best option.

P.S. If you feel you must check out a naked person's body (for one reason or another) please be sure not to get caught doing it. And avoid looking at the person *altogether* if you feel that involuntary ogling of genitalia is at all likely.

Dear Miss Mingle:

I have these two kind of rowdy college friends (they're both Texans), and when they visit me on the East Coast they tend to get a little wild. Anyway, one night they show up at my door in a stretch limo about the size of their home state. When I enter the car, I find them in the company of a completely nude, buxom blonde.

Miss Mingle, I am a married man, and believe it or not, beyond taking an occasional peek at my wife's Victoria Secret catalog, I have no real desire to touch or to otherwise sexually interact with any other woman. I know other guys might think I'm a wimp, but that's the way it is. So when I found myself in the car with this strange woman and my two leering friends, I felt very awkward and didn't know what to say to them—or to her. Should I have just tried to talk to her as if she were wearing clothes? What possible thing could I have said to her? Is it improper etiquette to ignore her, which is what I basically did?

Suffering From Overexposure

P.S. In case you are wondering, the four of us drove around drinking champagne for about an hour before I managed to excuse myself and go home while they continued on into what I assume was a night of at least mild debauchery.

Dear Suffering:

Call me a cynic, but somehow I can't quite believe you were all that miserable, although I am sure conversation was challenging for you, to say the least. Having never been a man, a Texan, or a prostitute, it is a little bit difficult for me to imagine the scene, but I'll give it a whirl, for the sake of naked women in limos everywhere.

I don't believe it is ever proper to ignore anyone in any social setting—even this one—unless they have badly insulted you or are threatening you, neither of which seems to have been the case here. I think the best stance to have taken would have been to have befriended the woman with a line like, "How can you stand these two characters?" and, if possible, to have shaken her hand in greeting. Other than being as polite to her as you could under the circumstances and excusing yourself as quickly as possible (an hour seems a little long for someone who is supposed to be suffering), there is nothing more you could do.

Except, of course, to permanently lose these rowdy so-called friends of yours!

Un-natural Disasters

The best laid plans can end in sudden calamity. Even for Miss Mingle.

When I was in college I did a lot of experimenting at parties. I'm not talking about drugs, I'm talking about mingling. One of my favorite tricks to liven up a dull party was to pretend I was a foreign studies student from Paris (give me a break, I was only nineteen). I couldn't speak much actual French but I had a pretty good French accent, and most people, I think, believed me. The act was fun, and men would flirt with me more than when I was just being me.

One night I was mingling away in my Parisian alter ego, feeling *absolument fabuleux*, when someone called out, "Hey Jeanne-Marie, somebody wants to meet you!"

I turned gaily, cigarette holder in hand, and was confronted by a dark, very handsome guy.

"Je suis Jacques Duplais," he said. "Vous êtes Parisienne?" And I realized with a horrible sinking feeling that he was really French!

I thought about trying to brave it out, but knew I would never make it. Everyone else was watching us, waiting for me to launch into my native tongue. "No, well, not really." I said in my normal voice. Then I just turned and fled.

Jeanne-Marie was never heard of again; and I learned that in mingling, as in life, the greater the fun, the greater the risk.

Dear Miss Mingle:

In recent years, because of my husband's business, he and I have been invited to many large gatherings. I have been getting pretty good at approaching strangers at these things. I pride myself on having perfected the technique where you ask people a lot of questions about themselves.

At one of these parties last week, I marched right up to a pregnant woman with the cheerful line, "Hello, you're just radiating from across the room. When is the little one due?" She looked confused at first and then, to my total horror and surprise, she blushed deeply and said, "Oh,...well...I'm not pregnant."

Miss, Mingle, what could I have done to get past this awful mistake I made?

Big Mouth Babe in Boston

Dear Big Mouth Babe:

If it makes you feel any better, this is one of the most common faux pas made. I usually advise people *never* to assume that any woman is pregnant, and not to say anything until she mentions it first. Even if she is so big she looks like she's having triplets. You just never know.

After the words are out, you can't take them back. What you can try to do is to smooth things over with a lie:

"Oh my God, I am so sorry—I was talking to someone about pregnancy and she pointed to you and told me you were expecting. I am absolutely horrified."

Or flattery:

"I *am* sorry. Really, it wasn't your weight, it was just this glow you have coming from you—you must be in love then, or something, to radiate like that."

Or just plead for mercy:

"I can't believe I said that to you. I feel terrible, I feel like jumping out the window, I just want to pull my tongue out. Will you please forgive me?"

However, as this is not only one of the most commonly made faux pas but also one of the worst, you may just want to cut your losses and fade away into another corner of the room.

Dear Miss Mingle:

I'm afraid have a terrible chronic party problem. I get so nervous whenever I am in a room with people I don't know that I invariably begin to giggle—and at the most inappropriate times. I don't have this problem at social functions where I know most of the people, only when there are a lot of strangers. Last week at a cocktail party, I started giggling right in the middle of someone telling me what they do for a living—and it wasn't a funny profession. I think the woman may have thought I was drunk. Can you help me, or do I need therapy?

The Giggler

Dear Giggler:

Ninety-five percent of America needs therapy; you probably don't need it more than anyone else does. In fact, minglephobia is a widespread disorder that people express in many different ways. Giggling or laughing at inappropriate times (otherwise known as laughing gaffes) is one of them. You might try to think of something very serious or sad when you get an attack of the giggles, like losing your job or your best friend. If that doesn't work you may have to resort to using one of the following lines:

"Excuse me; I always laugh a lot when I am having a good time. I can't help it."

"I'm only laughing because a psychic *told* me I was going to meet a [description of the person you are talking to] tonight!"

"Everyone in my family laughs when they are with someone very attractive."

"You must think I'm tipsy, but I am just really stressed out today and if I didn't laugh I'd cry!"

"I just came from the dentist and he gave me gas."

P.S. You could always just be honest and tell the person about your nervous habit. You'd be surprised how many people will empathize.

Encountering Celebrities

Trying to mingle among "the stars"—especially if you are not one—can be very intimidating. I'll never forget the evening I ran into my favorite actor from *L.A. Law*, John Spencer, at a Manhattan piano bar. When I spotted him my face lit up with a kind of goofy "Hey Wow!" expression, which he happened to see, much to my chagrin. From then on, every time he glanced my way I was either staring at him outright or stealing a furtive glance. I felt I couldn't go up and speak to him, as I might have done with an ordinary guy, because he was a celebrity and I didn't want to look like a star-struck fan. But that is, in fact, what I was.

After an hour, Mr. Spencer got up to leave. I was between him and the door and he was heading straight for my table. My heart began beating faster as he approached. Then, to my extreme excitement and delight, he stopped, right in front of me. He was looking down and smiling. I beamed back at him, and my mouth opened about half way. No sound came out. After several long seconds, the man took pity on me and very cordially put his hand out, which I accepted and shook.

Finally I found my tongue. "B-bye," I squeaked.

It's often hard to remember that celebrities are just people. And if the celebrity is an actor, it's even harder, because if you have seen him act, you feel as if you know him. You may even feel you have an emotional connection with him. But since he doesn't know you, it's weirdly one-sided—just like a childhood crush. And like a crush, it feels uncomfortable, and may do odd things to your heart rate and your facial muscles. You may babble incoherently or become, as I did, completely catatonic.

Dear Miss Mingle:

About nine years ago I became a fan of a certain musical celebrity—a huge fan. Two years ago I moved (for other reasons) to his hometown. Since then I have become very good friends with his wife, and my children play with his children. However, even though I am pretty outgoing, when I meet the celebrity at children's events, I become tongue-tied and stupid. How can I establish a "normal" relationship with this man and get over the awe of his fame? Every time we nod or smile at each other I get goose bumps.

Starstruck

Dear Starstruck:

Anything that gives you goosebumps can't be all bad. However, I know being tongue-tied is no fun. The more time you spend around this celebrity, the better it will get; the more you will be able to see him as just a normal guy. If his wife really has become a good friend, you could tell her how you feel and perhaps she would be willing to plan some social occasion that would give you more opportunity to have a conversation with him.

Here are Miss Mingle's seven secrets for holding one's own with any celebrity:

1. Always try to be prepared to run into a celebrity or an "important" person. (Note that the rules for celebrities can apply to corporate bosses, politicians or anyone you think is out of your social reach.) If you are not caught off guard you will fare better.

2. Breathe deeply, to help you stay relaxed.

3. Be respectful and admiring but not worshipful or gushy. The celebrity may welcome conversation with someone who doesn't *treat* him like a celebrity.

4. Remember that even celebrities have to go to the dentist. (If you can hold a mental picture of them in the chair, it helps reduce your nervousness.)

5. It sometimes works wonders for the conversation if you can fantasize that you too are a celebrity. If you are "equal" your words will flow more easily. (WARNING: Don't start bragging or trying to one-up the celebrity, however.)

6. When talking to a celebrity, compliment his per-

formance in his last movie or broadway show (if you've seen it) but then move on to other subjects, the way you would do with anyone else.

7. Project an attitude of not wanting to get anything from the celebrity, that you just thought it would be interesting to talk to him. Don't ask for the person's autograph, and don't hint around that you are hoping for an "in" into his field.

Net-Working:
Mingling in
Cyberspace

There are many truly amazing, wonderful, bizarre, and diverting things about the Internet, and one of them is mingling in cyberspace. It's almost frightening how many people you can contact with just a few touches of a button. You can even mingle with yourself, as radio talk show host Howard Stern found out when he went on line to check out the cyberspace scene and ran into a Howard Stern imposter.

But no matter how many people you are speaking with each day via the Net, no matter how many great

Websites you visit, please remember that it is, after all, still only the written word (okay, yes, with a lot of graphics decoration and some video elements), no matter how immediate the experience; and that nothing will ever, or should ever, replace "realspace" mingling. I had a horrible nightmare recently in which the traditional cocktail party had mutated into a cyberspace cocktail party, with all the guests sitting alone in front of their computer screens in darkened rooms, sipping martinis with one hand while moving their mouses with the other.

Needless to say, I woke up screaming.

Dear Miss Mingle:

I have a very bizarre confession to make. I am tongue-tied in cyberspace.

I like to cruise for men on-line. If I am on a bulletin board—no problem, I can talk about whatever the topic is. However, as I tend to pick the more esoteric boards such as "Favorite Women Artists—Except Georgia O'Keeffe" or "Research in Progress" or "Bay Area Cubs Fans." Often there is little straight male action on these bulletin boards. So then I will cruise the members directory, looking at profiles, choosing a potential E-male (Oops! I mean E-mail) dating partner. I have a list of names of single men who claim that they, too, like art and baseball. But how do I start a conversation with one of these guys out of the blue? How do I approach him without sounding like we are in a cyberspace fern bar? "Hey, I was checking out the members' profiles and I noticed you go to museums, too." Or "Hey, I was cruising through the directory and you sound like you like the same esoteric stuff I do"? My on-line tongue is virtually tied. Can you help me?

Lost in the Cyber-Surf

Dear Lost in the Cyber-Surf:

I don't think cruising the members directory is a very good strategy. First of all, cyberspace tends to be a fairly crude atmosphere, which is why many women remain anonymous on-line. A large percent of the people cruising the net are male, and the fact nobody can see them brings out the worst in some of them. As a result there seems to be a sort of locker-room syndrome in many arenas in cyberspace. If you are not careful, you are apt to run into a lot of semi-perverted heavy-breather types. Approaching men in the member's directory is worse than picking them up in bars; it's tantamout to randomly calling strange men on the phone. Secondly, much of the information in the profiles is complete fabrication, and you have no way of knowing what is and what is not the truth. It's true I am all for a little harmless make-believe while mingling, but that is when you can see and hear (and feel the energy of) the other person.

From what I understand about the cyber-Universe, it is far better to stick to chat rooms (in addition to bulletin boards) in subject areas you know or are interested in. If you find someone in the Bay-Area-baseball-lovers-Louis-XIV-furniture chat room who sounds interesting, you can let him know privately by sending him an IM (instant message), which will appear on his screen. Then you can continue a private conversation by E-Mail. The best opening line is usually something like: I REALLY LIKED WHAT YOU HAD TO SAY ABOUT JIM ABBOTT. LET'S TALK. I have heard that most chat rooms are mostly filled with inane babble, but if you can find one where the subject being discussed is highbrow and narrow enough, it can be fruitful. There are also areas available to place personal ads on most on-line services.

The thing you may be forgetting is that as exciting as the Internet is, it is not going to change the fact that when you approach a stranger, strange things may happen. Cyberspace is great but it can't change human nature. At least not yet.

Dear Miss Mingle:

I have been going to this new cyber-café down the street where you get coffee, pay a fee, and go on-line; and I must tell you I am a bit confused as to the rules of etiquette. For instance: Is it okay to strike up a conversation with the person sitting next to you (realspace) or are you supposed to stick to on-line interaction (cyberspace)? When you are in cyberspace, how do you know when someone is telling the truth, like when they tell you they are in a cyber-café in Paris? Is there some on-line lie detector system? Can I ask the person next to me for help or is that considered uncool? *And what are the rules about getting involved with what's going on on your neighbor's monitor?*

Cyber-Caf-fiend@.yea.moca

Dear Cyber-Caf-Fiend@.yea.moca:

Toto, I don't think we're in Kansas anymore.

APPENDIX

Miss Mingle's Emergency Guide to Social Survival